THE GAME OF LIFE!

A WOMAN'S GAME PLAN FOR SUCCESS

PATRICIA TAYLOR KENNEDY

THE GAME OF LIFE!

A WOMAN'S GAME PLAN FOR SUCCESS

Kennedy, Patricia Taylor. *The Game of Life! A Woman's Game Plan for Success*

All the events in this book are completely true, but to protect the identity and privacy of the individuals, all names and places have been changed.

The links included in this book were correct at the time of publication.

ISBNs: 979-8-9855314-0-4 (paperback), 979-8-9855314-1-1 (ebook)

Library of Congress Control Number: 2022914787

KWE Publishing, www.kwepub.com

Cover design by Michelle Fairbanks | Fresh Design

CONTENTS

Introduction   vii

SECTION I: THE PROBLEM
YOU DON'T KNOW THE GAME YOU'RE PLAYING

1. It's A Man's World   3
2. Operating System: Ages Zero to Seven   11
3. The Real World   17

SECTION II: THE NEGATIVE RESULT
NOT KNOWING THE GAME CREATES CONFUSION

4. Thinking Small   27
5. Not Knowing   35
6. Self-Doubt (Imposter Syndrome)   45

SECTION III: THE NEW RULES
HOW TO PLAY THE GAME OF LIFE

7. Creating a Vision for Your Life   55
8. Blueprint for Life: When You See It, You Can Be It   69
9. Opportunities, Not Tasks   79
10. Setting Boundaries   85

SECTION IV: THE NEW GAME
GET IN THE GAME

11. Soul Savings: Are You Willing to Invest?   91
12. Discipline: The World's Greatest Drug   97
13. The Four Pillars   107
14. Four Daily Activities for Success   113
15. Getting Clear   123
16. Break Down Plans into Manageable Pieces of Work   139
17. Planning   151
18. Just Say "No."   165
19. Self-Advocacy   175

20. How to Leverage Success   189
21. Self-Support   195

SECTION V: THE PLAY
TIPS FOR SUCCESSFUL GAME PLAY

22. Gratitude   207
23. Fear   217
24. Conclusion   223

About the Author   227
References   229

INTRODUCTION

"But I don't know what I want!" Agnes exclaimed as she threw her hands in the air in exasperation.

She looked at me. I was in a chair on the center-right side of the conference table, surrounded by a room full of young people at a Fortune 500 global company. I was training these employees on how to think about working with a mentor, how to show up for the meetings, and how to prepare themselves for success. As the creator of the entire program, the pressure was on me.

I was responsible for training the mentees in advance on how to work with a mentor, teaching the mentors how to lead, and organizing the kickoff event where everyone came together and met before pairing up. I created the worksheets; I had crafted the beautiful slide deck on the screen for them all to see. Heck, I even gave them pre-work and sample questions to ask their future mentors. There I was, in a room full of smart, promising, superstars who were seeking guidance and direction from me to help them move forward in their careers. All the faces in the room turned to me for an answer.

And I didn't know what to say.

Well in advance of this meeting, I had designed a lot of material, carefully crafted and planned the flow, and even thought of poten-tial questions the mentees might have. But I had not prepared for this one question: "What if I don't know what I want?" In a knee-jerk reaction, I frantically directed Agnes and the group to a personality test which also uncovers a person's strengths. Next, I suggested they focus on their strengths and consider the type of work that matches them. Then, the attendees could share those results with their assigned mentor who could help them figure out what focus areas might be best for them, career choices, roles they may wish to pursue where they would be a natural fit because of their strengths. When Agnes made her exclamation to the group, I knew deep down that there was more to Agnes's question than just knowing her strengths.

Then, it dawned on me. Like Agnes, I honestly did not know what I wanted either. There is no doubt that understanding your strengths is an important step in knowing who you are and learning what you are good at doing. Certainly, it helps, but as it turns out, knowing your strengths is only one part of the bigger puzzle.

After I went forward with the program, the majority of the participants indicated they were extremely happy with the results. Having a mentor help guide you in your career journey is an important part of managing your future, and research shows that it leads to success over your peers who do not have a mentor. But sometimes, even your mentor does not know how to dig in deeply and share a framework, a blueprint, on how to figure out your calling. In fact, I was a mentor, and I did not know how to do this for myself. I had read books, attended lectures, and listened to self-help folks who really helped me get clearer. But I had not reached that level of clarity where everything made sense. I did not know exactly where and why I was moving in a certain direc-tion in my career.

Gaining that understanding has to do with possibilities. Often, we look out into the world with a narrow focus of what is possible. Maybe you were a kid and wanted to be a basketball superstar when you grew up. Then, when you hit puberty, you only grew to be 5'7" in height. In addition, even though you practiced every single day, you were not talented enough to make it to the NBA. Maybe you wanted to be an actress or singer but didn't have the ability to sing. Or, even if you did have a good enough voice and pursued a performing career, you found you did not get the callbacks from auditions and were unable to break through. Your family and friends might have said to you, "At least you have a job to fall back on."

As we become adults, many of us do not even have those goals for ourselves and cannot come up with interests on our own other than choosing which degree sounds most interesting to us. This decision to choose a career path is frequently demanded of us at a point where we have no idea if that type of work is going to bring meaning into our lives. If we express uncertainty about which path to take, we are given a small array and told that those are our choices—those degrees. *Which one do you want? Pick one and go get a job after you graduate. Make money and start a family.* Where is the meaning in that?

We hear those stories, that same advice all the time, so it beats us down. Maybe instead of chasing our dreams, we just look at jobs that are available, and we fit ourselves into that box and move forward. I know because I have lived that life. I found myself in a box with a limited view, without looking outside the structure I had placed around myself in terms of possibilities. It is soul-crushing.

While choosing a career path can be difficult for all people, it is especially difficult for women. In the game of life, expectations are different for girls who grow into the women who enter the workforce. In the years that women have been in the workforce, barriers have been broken, and we've had advantages previous generations haven't had. Yet the workforce we are in runs mainly by rules created by men.

It's a man's world, and I want to share with you the reasons why it is so and what you as a woman can do. I intend for you to read this book and walk away knowing, "I can create my own rules of this workforce game to set a path for ME!"

Who am I to give this advice? First, I am a single mom past the middle-career stage in a Fortune 500 company where I've recently had experience in project management, but I'm also, a Women in Leadership coach, mentor, and mentorship programming Leader. I am a career and life coach.

My background includes being in project management, a scrum master, mentorship program creator, sales leader, trainer, small business owner, and the list goes on. For a short period of time, I was a flight attendant too. Throughout those careers, I was chasing my dreams, looking for the right place for me. When I had children, things changed. I started my own small business, which rewarded my soul. But when I divorced, I let that business go and went right back into corporate America, making survival choices to make ends meet. That is what many of us do every single day. There was not much meaning in my career other than supporting my family, which is incredibly important.

But there was still something missing for me. My kids will grow up and I will always be their mom, but then what is next? Where will my calling be? Is that all there is?

Prompted by Agnes as I pondered my next steps in my career, I thought about Maslow's hierarchy of needs. I thought I was a fully actualized person and, if that were true, why I had I not figured this part out? For those of you who are not familiar, Abraham Maslow became popular during the 1950s as one of the founders and driving forces within humanistic psychology. His theories included the hierarchy of needs, self-actualization, and peak experiences. He basically stated that you must have these foundational aspects in place before you could be a self-actualized person. Thinking about that framework, I looked at my own life. Before that day in the conference room, I thought I had the foundations in place and was even giving back by starting mentorship programs to help others. But I still felt like something was missing. I wondered about the answer to the question, "What is my true calling?"

Well, how was that possible? I thought to myself, *I am self-actualizing, aren't I? Why can't I answer the basic question of how to find purpose in my life? Isn't my purpose helping others find mentors so they can determine their life goals? Wait a minute...*

I realized the reason I was creating mentorship programs for others was because I was searching for purpose in my life too! BLAM! That was a huge insight into my drivers. I thought to myself, *Now what do I do?*

Learning from my insights about my point of realization and education is where this book can help. This book walks you through the strategies, techniques, and practices that empowered me. You will benefit from the years of study, research, and practice that I embarked upon, where I tried and failed, and more in my journey to determine what I wanted out of life. Reading this book and implementing the actions I found helpful will help you save time. Most importantly, the lessons you learn in this book will help you to be successful in your life.

What you are about to discover in reading this book is that life is a game of sorts. In fact, to be successful in life, it is important to understand where it is you want to go. The problem is that most of us do not know where it is we want to go in life.

When you see celebrities on television, in movies, and on social media you may think, *That is what my life is supposed to be!* And then, social media makes you feel guilty because you are not wealthy, and you think that even if you were to pursue making money as a goal, you would find it to be empty and without meaning. Instead, you might feel bad about yourself for not living the dream (even when you know less than 1% of people have the means to live the way life is portrayed on social media). That myth of the good life that we see everywhere not only makes us feel bad about ourselves but confuses us even more because we never figure out this game.

As a young woman in business, I was stunned to learn I was metaphorically playing checkers in my career while the men at work were playing chess. As a result, I ended up with self-doubt, felt bad, and moved even further from achieving the meaningful life I deserved. I didn't start succeeding until I figured out what game I was playing.

No one gives you a rule book to follow when you are a parent. Nor do they give you one as a teenager that you can use as a guide to be successful in high school and beyond. There isn't a rule book for women once you graduate college and step out into the world on your own, either.

But now there is.

Once I learned there is a framework, a strategy you can create, and things you can do to understand and create meaning in your life, I wanted to shout it from the rooftops.

Wouldn't you like to figure out what you want to do in a way that will give you hope, joy, and meaning?

With your decision to read this book, I hope your answer is "yes!" I want to give you the framework in this book to accomplish this goal. It is up to you to learn, study, and do the work. Once you do, then you too will achieve what the lucky few are able to achieve: peace, mindfulness, a purpose in their lives, meaning, and much more. Does this mean you will attain riches? It might. For many people, finding the answer to those questions creates more than enough internal riches and gratitude that money cannot buy.

As women, we have a lot of societal expectations that are

confusing and do not set us up for success. Many times, we cannot even see these things that stand in our way, but they do exist. There are some areas that are addressed in this book that will help you to see more clearly the landscape in which you find yourself.

Just like knowing how to play a game so you are best positioned to win, understanding the Game of Life will help position you for success. You will learn the landscape in which you are playing and understand the game itself. I want to share those insights with you, dear reader, so that you can rise up and have incredible success in your life.

However, all of it is up to you.

Are you ready to learn the Game of Life? Buckle up, here we go!

SECTION I: THE PROBLEM
YOU DON'T KNOW THE GAME YOU'RE PLAYING

CHAPTER 1
IT'S A MAN'S WORLD

I'm a mother to two daughters. When my two children were born, I was dedicated to trying to make a difference by coaching and mentoring women to think bigger and go for desired promotions and higher salaries. From my thirties onward, I was an advocate for women's rights.

Now that my girls are adults, it is disappointing to learn that the disparity in pay and in executive roles still exists. Not much progress has occurred. Ever heard the phrase—or even the song —"It's A Man's World" by James Brown? Well, it still is a man's world, and things are certainly changing, but not fast enough.

Compared to men, women in 2020 took home an annual salary equivalent to 82.3%. With women of color, the gap widens even further. Studies showed women earning just 57 cents per dollar as compared to their male counterparts in 1973, and sadly closing this pay gap is still out of our reach today.[1]

Even worse, a Pew Research Center survey conducted in 2017 found about four in ten working women (42%) said they had experienced gender discrimination at work, as compared with about two-in-ten men (22%). Earnings inequality was one of the most commonly reported forms of discrimination. While only 5% of men said they had earned less than a woman doing the same job, the research uncovered that one in four employed women said they had earned less than a man who was doing the same job.[2]

At this rate, we as women will not likely break even with the pay gap until 2050. What can we do in order to change this statistic once and for all? The obvious answer is to ask for a salary to match your worth. In order to do that, you must start by knowing your worth. The problem is that many women do not know how valuable they are and gladly accept what they can get.

How are we able to compete when the playing field is not level? Step 1 is to know the landscape. Realize the game is set up for you to remain several steps behind. Let's look at the facts.

On the ladder to success, women often do not have that first rung. I am speaking in general terms as there are always exceptions. However, most women on their corporate career ladders never rise up. Why is that?

Here are some statistics from the 2019 McKinsey report. Please see graphic below.

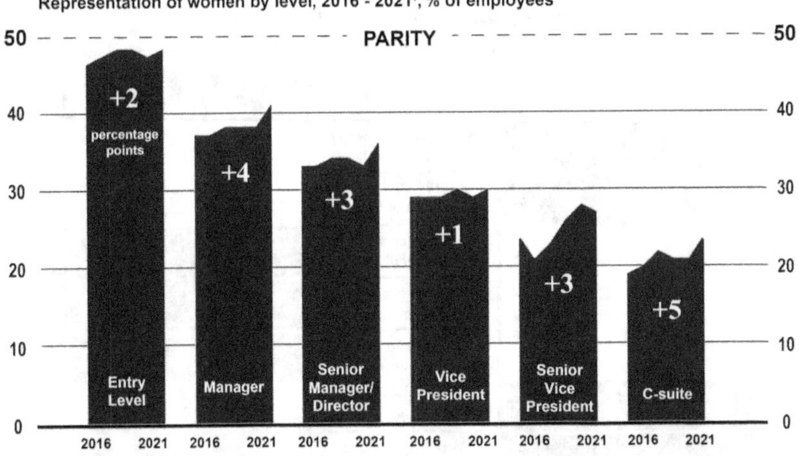

The previous chart is showing us that we are half the population, and in major corporations, the ratio of women to men is close to 50%. So why are 80% of C-Suite roles still filled with men? It should be close to 50% women and 50% men, not 80% men and less than 20% women. Why are we still here? What isn't happening?

For starters, the C-Suite and Sr Manager up to C-Suite role split is not going to happen by itself. I've been waiting years for changes to take place and the changes in my lifetime have been very small and, in some cases, it is stagnant or going backward.

Please refer to the chart shown below to see just how small the changes have been.

A look back shows where companies have made progress - and where more needs to be done.

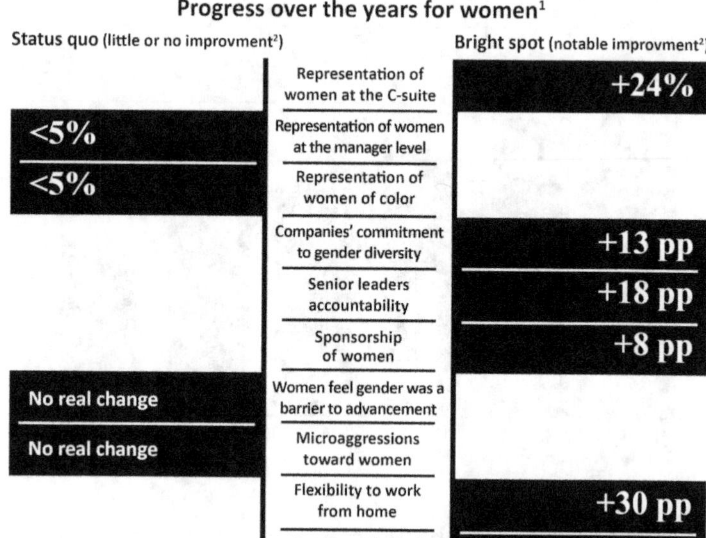

[1]Where 2015 data was not available, best historical data was used instead for comparison.
[2]Changes reflected in either percent change for representation or percentage points (pp).
Source: 2019 McKinsey & Company and LeanIn.Org Women in the Workplace study.

We have not come as far as I had hoped. I wanted a better future for my daughters when they were young. In general, I wanted better opportunities for women in the workplace. It is 20+ years later, and not much has changed.

It is important to be aware of the biases you might face in the workplace. That McKinsey study mentioned above basically states that for every 100 men who get promoted, only 70 women get promoted. McKinsey goes on to note that hiring managers only hire women who have achieved the skills they are hiring for in the past while they turn around and hire men on the potential they see in them. That statement is one of the most frustrating to me because, in the past, I thought I was always being considered because of what hiring managers saw in terms of my potential.[3]

What do we do? We have to be the change we want to see in this world. If women do not step up and advocate for themselves, create plans and execute them to make this change happen, then it simply won't. We cannot depend upon men to open the door for us. We must take it upon ourselves to enact the change we want to see in this world.

The only advice that McKinsey suggests is that we teach leaders of organizations how to be less biased. I have two grown daughters, and I am tired of waiting for things to change, quite frankly. What I would suggest to all the women who wish to climb the corporate ladder is to start by seeing what is happening. Reading this book and incorporating the suggestions shared will go a long way toward standing up for yourself because you will recognize the biased decisions/actions more clearly. For example, stand up for yourself in meetings when you speak up and no one acknowledges your comment. Speak up for other women when you witness the same actions taking place toward them. We must support and encourage each other.

Recognize the biases that you see. Study what those biases are. That's the first step to learning how to mitigate them. Be aware that a majority of what people exhibit, whether it is the words they say or the actions they demonstrate, is based on unconscious bias. We all have unconscious biases. According to the University California Irvine School of Biological Sciences, "Unconscious biases are social stereotypes about certain groups of people that individuals form outside their own conscious awareness. Everyone holds unconscious beliefs about various social and identity groups, and these biases stem from one's tendency to organize social worlds by categorizing." People judge others based on their own preferences. In a recruiting scenario, choosing someone who has similar interests as you or who went to the same school can lead to unconscious bias. For example, a hiring manager prefers a job applicant that is a fan of the same football team. Initially, that doesn't sound unreasonable until you look at that hiring manager's all-male team, each of whom is a fan of that same football team. It may not be that blatant in your company, but these inherent preferences can lead to a lack of workplace diversity.

Watch people's actions and do not give too much credence to their words. The old saying "actions speak louder than words" is an accurate phenomenon. Here are some examples of what it might look like:

Gender bias in recruiting and pay—ensure you set gender-neutral standards for recruiting. For example, make certain panels of interviewers are diverse in gender and race. Analyze the new hires against the interviewees across the organization to determine if certain panels favor men over women or certain races over others. The goal is an equitable distribution. The same can be said of salaries. Women still get paid 82 cents on the same dollar men get paid (this is as of the latest research conducted as of the writing of this book). Ensure your HR leaders are analyzing the salaries to make certain women are equitably compensated.

There is another important unconscious bias that takes place even today. I have experienced it myself, and I go into a deeper dive on this topic later in the book. Women tend to get tasks while men get opportunities. When you look at projects or assignments that are delegated to you, are you getting task-driven assignments or projects that make a measurable impact on the organization? In other words, is this new assignment or project something that will help make a case for your next promotion or is it organizing a team outing? Recognize where you might be getting stereotypical assignments rather than true opportunities. Please focus on the descriptions provided later in this book to learn how to ensure you are getting the right exposure and experience.

Next, let's talk about starting your own company if that turns out to be your life's purpose. Remember that McKinsey study? They also determined that women's jobs are 1.8 times more at risk than men's. Therefore more women leave corporate roles, and some are trying to start their own firms. According to *Harvard*

Business Review, in 2019, 2.8% of funding went to women-led star-tups; in 2020, that fell to 2.3%. [4]

To level the playing field, we have to know the game we are playing. Therefore, it is important to look at the known issues and understand the root causes before we can start changing the world. We need to know more about the landscape. Let's explore how we were raised and how those elements add to the reasons why we have not achieved gender parity.

I would ask that you take the time to read through this book, get clear on what you want to achieve in your life, and take on those tasks and goals that align with your mission. This is your life, and you do have the ability to reach for the stars if that is the direction in which you wish to go. The purpose of this book is to encourage you to learn as much as possible so that you recognize the things that do not serve you over the long run, which ulti-mately enables you to create the life you desire.

---

1. 2020 Bureau of Labor statistics. https://blog.dol.gov/2021/03/19/5-facts-about-the-state-of-the-gender-pay-gap#:~:text=Women%20earn%2082%20-cents%20for,for%20many%20women%20of%20color.
2. 2017 Pew Research Center survey, https://www.pewresearch.org/fact-tank/2021/05/25/gender-pay-gap-facts/
3. McKinsey.com, A look back shows where companies have made progress—and where more needs to be done. https://www.mckinsey.com/~/me-dia/mckinsey/featured%20insights/gender%20equali-ty/women%20in%20the%20workplace%202019/svgz-women-in-the-workplace-2019-infographic.svgz
4. Harvard Business Review, 2019. https://hbr.org/2021/02/women-led-star tups-received-just-2-3-of-vc-funding-in-2020

CHAPTER 2

OPERATING SYSTEM: AGES ZERO TO SEVEN

If you regularly use a computer, you know there is only so much memory available. To operate your computer effectively, things like saving documents, maintaining the current time, etc., are all done automatically. No one must manually click a button to change the date or set the time. You don't have to think about it. The computer simply acts on your behalf.

Similar to a computer, human brains have an operating system that is established when we are between the ages of zero to seven years old. This means that between that age range, we learn how we are supposed to act in the world. That operating system is what we keep using as adults unless we become aware of it and do work to install a different belief (program).

Essentially, all of your beliefs about people, family, relationships, money, your potential, and more were created in your mind between the ages of zero to seven. Dr. Bruce Lipton describes this operating system as Theta. Theta is your subconscious mind. It operates in the background without you having to consciously think about it.[1]

Between zero to seven years of age, your mind is a sponge,

picking up everything around you, observing animals, people, the world, television, books, and more. If you learn dogs are fun to be around because you have a family pet, then most likely you will not be afraid of dogs when you get older. That belief that dogs are friendly has been installed in your operating system. But if you get bitten by a dog early on, you might have learned dogs are mean and scary and that you cannot trust them. That program stays with you for life unless you consciously change it.

In most cases, what we learn during these formative years is simply taken in. Often, there is no context, and we do not understand all the nuances in play. We see what happened, and that becomes the way we view the world going forward unless we change our views. (There are always exceptions and special circumstances, so please note that what I am describing is for illustrative purposes to help you understand how we develop and why we act the way we do in some cases.)

As we become adults, our subconscious is partly to blame if we are experiencing struggles in our lives. Let's use the example of learning early on that all dogs are scary. As an adult, you might want to date a man who loves dogs, but your fear stops you. As much as you might want to be around his dog, you struggle because it feels too scary. No matter how much evidence there is that this dog is friendly and nice, you feel you cannot overcome your fears. That is your operating system at work. It is trying to protect you because it learned all dogs are scary. Therefore, it will take conscious effort to unlearn that belief that was instilled into your unconscious.

In many cases, what you learned was a protection mechanism designed to keep you safe. The problem is that the programming you picked up in those early years might be causing you internal anguish. It might even be blocking you from achieving success.

For example, if you were told in school by a teacher in front of everyone in the classroom that you shouldn't act bossy and you agreed with her and were deeply ashamed of how you behaved, then that experience gets stored in your operating system. Now as an adult, anytime you speak up, especially in a public setting, you make especially sure that you don't come across as "bossy" and are unlikely to speak up at all. How many times have you seen women who sit quietly in meetings and rarely raise their hand or speak up? This type of behavior could be attributed to what they learned as they were growing up. Given this understanding of how women are shaped by society, it becomes clear to see how limited we become—even in our actions.

Even though as adults we continue to operate based on the programming that we accumulated between the ages of zero to seven, we are not always aware of it. This behavior is similar to being on autopilot when driving to work. Since you have driven to work so many times, you can think of other things while driving, and suddenly, you arrive at work without being aware of it. Has that happened to you? You don't have to think about turning on the turn signal or braking at a stop light; you automatically just do it.

In a similar fashion, our brains work that way with all the information we pick up between the ages of zero to seven. Therefore, it is easy to not even notice when you are acting in a manner in which you would rather not. Have you ever shouted at someone who cut you off in traffic? No one can hear you unless there are passengers with you. This reaction is not in our best interest. It raises our blood pressure, makes us anxious, and can put us on a path of being angry for the rest of our trip. Sometimes, we think that everyone reacts this way and never stop to think that there might be a better way to handle that type of situation. While that is true, I believe the better way to view it is, *That person must be late for work and is having a bad morning.* Then, think of ways to not let it get to the point of actually shouting out loud. If we are honest with ourselves, we know that the odds are fairly high that someone will cut us off at some point while driving in rush hour traffic. So why would we continue to allow ourselves to react in such an aggressive manner each time it occurs? How might we think about this situation in advance? We can realize that the other person is having a bad day and remain calm so our blood pressure doesn't become elevated and retain our composure.

This is also true for times when we might get angry at a significant other because the kitchen is not clean, and we have to make dinner and are hungry. You might get upset and take it out on your partner instead of thinking, *I noticed that I tend to get angry when I don't get my needs met rather than simply asking for what I want.* Have you gotten mad when your needs weren't met? I certainly have. It stems from being a child when my parents would reply to my request for something in a negative manner. Does this mean they are bad people? Of course not! But when this continues to happen because your mom has two other children to care for and is trying to clean the house for a guest to come over for lunch, sometimes answers are curt and unexpected. If it happens frequently, you learn that you will not get your needs met when you ask. This is a very simplified example and an important one because there are tons of these instances that occurred as we were growing up, and our child minds decided that this was how the world works. We've been operating that way ever since, meaning we learned to not get our needs met and not even ask.

Let's take this a few steps further. When you were young, you likely watched cartoons on television with stories and characters like Cinderella or Snow White. You learned from these shows that women have a certain role to play, and you believed that this was how it was. You might have had a brother who liked to watch action hero cartoons where he learned that boys were supposed to be tough, and they fought to save the world. How many cartoons showed girls saving the world when you were young? In my case, very few.

Therefore, all the television programming to which we were

exposed also programs us to believe women take care of children, cook, and need to be protected. We also learned to look to men to protect us and take care of us instead of us learning to be independent and take care of ourselves. All of this societal programming adds to our unconscious belief systems and helps to perpetuate the world in which we find ourselves—where men earn more money and have most of the executive jobs in most companies. They feel entitled to it due to their social upbringing, and everything is in place to welcome them into the club, so to speak. As women, our social conditioning sometimes prevents us from even envisioning that it is possible for us to achieve the same success, and we pull ourselves out of the game before it has even begun. Further, our societal conditioning keeps us in place. This cultural conditioning is designed for the benefit of others, not for ourselves.

Isn't it time to change? Of course it is! It is important to reflect upon actions that trigger you to act badly and define a new way to handle your reactions instead of being triggered and acting badly. We will always get triggered but that does not mean we have to react in ways we wish we hadn't.

---

1. https://capitalistcreations.com/youve-got-some-looming-childhood-issues/

CHAPTER 3
THE REAL WORLD

As a child, your instilled operating system is established when you are too young to accurately understand and make sense of the circumstances. Next, you start school, and an entirely new set of rules begins to emerge.

As a result of the structure of the world in which we live, our societal norms and cultures create a certain definition of who women are and how we should act. We think small and do not even realize it.

The world beats you down and helps to keep you in a box. How does this happen? Our parents might have told us as girls how we should act: "That's not ladylike" or "Don't act so bossy, no one will like you" are just a few examples. You may have heard other sayings that parents say to their children to maintain the gender norm to ensure their children remain inside the lines someone else has drawn for them. "Girls should not play football" or "Don't play so rough" are a few more types of comments that shape what we ourselves believe we are capable of achieving. Even in the newspaper articles that draw attention to the fact that many more women are playing football, many of the articles' point of view is that the premise of a female playing the game is shocking. If you read the article, the stance is that they appear shocked that a female player can actually be successful. The articles announce it as if it is the first time a female has ever done so when there are hundreds of girls playing football in our high schools today. When parents follow social norms while parenting their children, it is not done out of a place of intentional harm but rather to protect children from the ostracism they might face if that child acts differently than everyone expects. However well-meaning it is, this phenomenon starts to shape you as a child and you learn to live your life with the same beliefs. Then, when you go to school, teachers reinforce the societal norms for boys and girls.

Studies have shown teachers often call on boys more than girls to answer questions in the classroom, creating inherent biases that shape women as we are growing up. It continues throughout our lives. There are studies that back this up. Once aware, teachers purposely change their behavior, but there are numerous studies supporting this statement. In a 2018 article[1], teachers were recorded in classrooms. The teachers even knew they were being videotaped. "Only a few studies have used videotapes to look at gender bias in teacher classroom practice(e.g., Davis 2000; Sadker and Sadker, 1994). Sadker and Sadker analyzed videotapes in the fourth, sixth, and eighth grades in four states and the District of Columbia in the USA. Their analysis showed the following:

1. Teachers interacted more with boys than with girls.
2. Boys received more praise, criticism, and remediation than girls.
3. During a discussion, boys were eight times more likely than girls to call out (shout out answers even when not called on).
4. Teachers were less likely to reject behavior by boys, even if it violated classroom rules. (The teachers'

rationale was that the boys tended to be more demanding and that their tones and attitudes obliged teachers to respond.)

5. Girls received more "acceptance" (a bare acknowledgment of their work, such as "uh-huh" or "okay") than boys.
6. Girls who received less attention from their teachers may have come to underestimate their abilities and lose motivation."

Then, there is the playground. Girls are told we are not supposed to get dirty, and we are not supposed to act "bossy" or in any way that is outside of the boundaries of how the society says girls should act. If you do, the other children will call you out —to the entire playground—and you will feel ostracized. Since most humans are communal creatures, we obey these unwritten laws and become compliant. How is one supposed to know themselves if they were prevented from exploring their boundaries— their own, not societal ones?

As girls move into the preteen ages of life, they start to depend on their peers more so than their parents for guidance. In this phase, many young girls begin to rely heavily on what others think of them rather than their own sense of self. On the happy path, young girls gain independence from their families and grow up to be resilient young women with a strong sense of self. On the other side of that spectrum, girls can develop insecurities that remain with them their entire lives. According to Dosomething.org, "75% of girls with low self-esteem reported engaging in negative activities like cutting, bullying, smoking, drinking, or disordered eating." Contrast this to only 25% of girls who have high self-esteem. Before they become adults, approximately 20% of teens will experience depression.[2]

The cited experts go on to state that "seven in ten girls believe that they are not good enough or don't measure up in some way, including their looks, performance in school, and relationships with friends and family members," and that "[a] girl's self-esteem is more strongly related to how she views her own body shape and body weight than how much she actually weighs." These mistaken beliefs carry on into adulthood. No wonder so many women feel the effects of what is commonly known as "Imposter Syndrome," where people do not believe they are good enough.

Women are taught, shaped by society, and reinforced in media to behave, look, and dress in a certain way in order to be acceptable. We wear makeup, high heels, etc., to fit into a societal norm, not realizing it is created by someone else's set of standards, not our own.

Life for women in this world is different than it is for men. When we start out in life, we are told to not get our dresses dirty, not to speak too loudly, and to be nice to others, whereas men are taught when they are young that they should toughen up. They learn as boys that it is not only ok but expected that they will play outside and get dirty. From early on, expectations shape all of us. As women, we accept these societal norms and do not realize that when we are grown up, we can change them, which expands our idea of what's possible more broadly.

During our childhood and teen years, we are also taught our value in this world. For example, if our parents continually tell us we are no good, we believe it. Some of us react in such a way to prove we ARE good. We might get angry and think, *I'll show you,* and go out of our way to prove our parents wrong. This might show up as an unhealthy pattern, like succeeding at all costs. In the long run, those of us who go out of our way to prove our parents wrong do not find satisfaction in our successes.

Others believe their parents and take on the mantra of not being good. Parents also might say no to a field trip because "we can't afford it." Based on this scenario, children might feel rejected and assume that they are not worth the investment. This rejection might teach those children they are not valuable enough to spend money on for school trips. This is just one example of how children learn to operate in life based on their childhood experiences and their interpretations of the world.

This happens to boys and girls; no one is immune. The problem is that most of us do not re-write the programming because we are not even aware that it exists. As a result, many of us grow into adults with mistaken beliefs and insecurities. We go into adulthood thinking we are "fine" and start to get jobs, enter relationships, start having children, and never stop to think about ourselves and our beliefs. We never question our upbringings or challenge these mistaken beliefs because most adults are operating from the same or similar mistaken beliefs.

When we enter adulthood, we seek people who are similar in thought to us and become friends. Some of us find friends who have different perspectives on life, and we learn from them. Many of us simply flock to people who are like us and do not learn different perspectives nor consider alternative viewpoints. If everyone around us (or at least the people to whom we gravitate) operate in a similar way, how would we know something is amiss? We are often more likely to bond because we feel comfortable with another woman who is just as insecure about her body and looks as we are. This bond keeps us stuck in our negative self-image. It is what we are familiar with, and often, we do not take the time to question these beliefs.

Most of us do not realize the extent to which insecurities are driving our decisions, such as the jobs to which we aspire (or do not). Our friend choices keep us stuck in our thinking because they reinforce our inner thoughts, such as, *Who do you think you are trying to get a job like that?* or worse.

In addition to career pressure, many people marry because they feel pressure to pair up and have children. It is instilled in many of us from an early age that we are supposed to grow up, go to college (for some of us), get a job, get married, and have kids. Happily ever after. But too often, the partner we seek is not someone we have thought about from a healthy perspective. We seek the familiar. Even when we choose a mate, heterosexual women gravitate towards men who resemble their fathers. Interestingly this applies even to women who are adopted. Data demonstrated that heterosexual women model their ideal spouse by using their dads as a template, a process called "sexual imprinting," according to Tamas Bereczkei and colleagues at the University of Pécs.[3]

According to an article in *Psychology Today*, a German psychologist named Julia Onken has identified three main strategies heterosexual women use to gain love and attention from males:

1. Pleasing males with their looks and/or their good-girl behavior ('I please, therefore I am').
2. Impressing males with their performance and success ('I accomplish, therefore I am').
3. Defying males ('I get negative attention, therefore I am').

While combining these approaches works too, most women choose one strategy that becomes dominant. Attempting to gain a man's affection by pleasing them is the most popular because this approach is the least threatening and most often presented in advertisements which are male-dominated.[4]

This conditioning is the foundation upon which we make our lifelong decisions. It is flawed. We do not have to prove our worth to be marriage material. We should not spend our lives focused on "pleasing our man" to our own detriment. Unless we realize that we are making partner choices based on a false construct, we will never grow out of this false narrative.

Is it any wonder why we aren't happy?

———————————————

1. Springer Open, "Failing to notice? Uneven teachers' attention to boys and girls in the classroom." https://izajole.springeropen.com/articles/10.1186/s40172-018-0069-4

2. DoSomething.org, "Eleven Facts about Teens and Self-Esteem," https://www.dosomething.org/us/facts/11-facts-about-teens-and-self-esteem#:~:text=75%25%20of%20girls%20with%20low,depression%20before%20they%20reach%20adulthood

3. New Scientist, "Women Marry Men Who Look Like Dad," https://www.newscientist.com/article/dn4928-women-marry-men-who-look-like-dad/#:~:text=Women%20tend%20to%20choose%20husbands,P%C3%A9cs%20in%20Hungary%20and%20colleagues.

4. Psychology Today, "Help, I Married My Father," https://www.psychologytoday.com/us/blog/unified-theory-happiness/201707/help-i-married-my-father

SECTION II: THE NEGATIVE RESULT

NOT KNOWING THE GAME CREATES CONFUSION

CHAPTER 4
THINKING SMALL

The game Monopoly™ is centered on real estate economics. The purpose of the game is to buy as many properties on the board as possible and put others out of business with no way to earn money. If you are successful in buying a majority of the properties, then the only way for your competitors to remain in the game is to keep paying you money for landing on your property. That is how you win.

When I was first learning how to play Monopoly™, however, my programming told me that I did not want to be mean to others and not give them a chance to buy real estate for themselves. My operating system kept me from winning. I never won the game until I stopped being charitable and made the goal of winning at all costs come first and foremost.

Knowing the object of the game is important if your goal is to win. That way, you understand more fully all the things that might prevent you from winning.

We think our world is made up of the "college, career, marriage, family, retire, die" paradigm, right?

Well, some of us know that there is more to life, but let's start at that basic paradigm. What have we done if we believe that all there is to life is that pathway? Well, we have placed ourselves into a box. There is an entire world outside that box, but you dare not look out there, go out there, be different, be expressive, and be yourself. But I thought, *No, no, no, not for me. I am successful inside the box, doing all the right things, staying inside the lines, and living societal norms.*

I liked to think that I was not in a box. I was aware that there were folks who existed outside of the box, and I was even friends with them, and they were successful. But I thought, *No, no, no, not for me. I am successful inside the box, and I am doing all the right things, staying inside the lines, living societal norms.* All the while, I was wondering why I didn't fit in. Why was I unhappy? How come my life felt so empty? Oh, sure, I'd have moments of happiness and joy in my life, but doing the daily grind loses its brightness over time. So, I volunteer to ensure I get the experiences important to me. I led a Girl Scout troop and arranged experiences for them that were way outside the normal patch requirements that enriched their lives and opened them to new possibilities. That was rewarding and meaningful. But my job situation left me feeling empty, and trying to justify my job as being rewarding is tiresome. I'd done it for years!

There I was in my life, fitting into the box, convincing myself I was NOT in the box, always looking outward and attracted to friends and people who are outside of the proverbial box. Trying to get into their minds to see what they knew that I didn't. But it turns out, there's little difference between what they knew and what I knew.

Here's the bottom line: unless you have done your soul-searching, sat down, and really worked at uncovering YOUR answers to the questions that lead to a more meaningful life, you might find yourself unfulfilled, too, whether you buy into the limiting life belief or not.

We are conditioned to only look out at the world from the

perspective of being in a box. This box is what society, our parents, friends, teachers, and more have said to us or reinforced in us. As a girl, you are expected to act and think in a certain way to be accepted. This programming happens to boys, too. We all are subject to this reinforcement of who we are supposed to be because of our gender. Then, the net result is that we grow up thinking we are the person we were told to be. But it is not. You might have a deep feeling of being conflicted and not sure why you feel that way. Essentially, you have been placed in a box that society tells you to stay inside of—or else. You have already met the consequences of not staying inside the box—when your friends tell you to wear makeup, style your hair a certain way, or wear certain clothes, etc.

When you are inside of a box, you cannot see very far because it limits your view. When your view is limited, you create only from the confines of the box.

There are examples of training elephants from a very young age to stay in place by tying one of their legs to a chain that limits how far they can go. Once they reach a certain age, they stop trying to go beyond the area the chain limited them to. They never realize when they are adults that they can rip the chain up out of the ground and walk wherever they wish. Instead, they are conditioned to remain in place. The shocking reality is that we are similar to these elephants with all our limiting beliefs we've acquired throughout our lives.

There is a great article on Inc.com referencing how limiting beliefs that we learn when we are very young hold us back over our lifetimes, similar to how young elephants are trained to remain in place. [1]

This phenomenon happens to both women and men, and understanding these concepts will help everyone reimagine a life that they wish to create—outside of the box placed upon them. My perspective is from my personal experience as a woman. I was taught that you shouldn't go to college unless you want to become a doctor or a lawyer. The implied message also was that I was going to get married, and the years spent on a degree would be a waste of time. That was a belief I took on even though I loved learning.

When I went to earn my bachelor's degree in my late twenties, I was embarrassed because there were so many people younger than I was, and I was ashamed that I waited so long to get my degree. But I pursued it anyway because I saw that I could have access to a better future just by having a degree. In addition, the people I met and the courses I truly enjoyed taking all opened my mind up to more possibilities. The more people I met, the more interesting life became. The more perspectives I could see, the more my life was broadened, and then the more interesting it became. I started to volunteer as a docent at the New York Botanical Gardens, which opened up even more growth and possibilities for me.

The more I did, and the more exposure I had to different views, cultures, jobs, and experiences, the more I grew as a person. I realized that I could be so much more than what I had initially thought I could be.

It is important to understand the landscape of careers/jobs/societal expectations for women. Being raised as a woman in our society ill prepares us for playing the career game. Once we are made aware, we can decide if we want to play inside the box that is created for women or if we wish to create another landscape, one that we define as ours. For example, now that I know the landscape in the game of Monopoly^{TM}, I can decide to lose if I do not wish to take everyone's opportunities away from them or simply decide not to play the game. In that same way, each of us can determine our goals for ourselves, but unless we know the landscape, we might be making decisions in the dark.

One insidious reason why opportunities are taken away is that women in business are made busy with tasks that lead nowhere. Look around at the assignments you are given at work. How many of the assignments on which you are working actually lead to opportunities?

Learn to say "no" to those tasks that do not lead to a career move. Now, let me be clear—in most roles, there are tasks that are part of our jobs. Those come with the territory. I am talking about the over and above work. Seek out those assignments that are hard and reap high rewards. Volunteering makes sense to do because it can help you get experience you might not have gotten otherwise. But think about it from a strategic career position and ask yourself, "How will this advance my career?" If it does not, politely decline. Tasks to consider might include assignments that expand your network and provide senior-level visibility or ones that help build key strengths. When helping to prepare for a workshop entitled "Barrier Busters," which was about bias in the workplace with two other amazing women, I was encouraged to listen to a Ted Talk by Sara Sanford called "How to Design Gender Bias Out of Your Workplace" about gender equality. While Sanford mentioned several examples, the phrase that stuck with me was, "Women get tasks. Men get opportunities." The team I worked with also cited several examples from a McKinsey report researchers refer to as the "Broken Rung," which is getting even worse due to Covid-19. That worsening is also because childcare at home primarily falls onto the shoulders of women, and they must take a step back from their careers.[2]

But this idea of women getting tasks struck a chord that deeply resonated with me. When I first watched the video of Ms. Sanford speaking about this issue, I simply thought it was an interesting premise. But then, I looked around, and I suddenly saw it in action everywhere I turned. I realized it had taken place my entire career. While women were working on volunteer-type tasks or tasks that simply needed to get done, men were getting opportunities that grew their careers.

I went through my memory banks and remembered all the task-type work assigned to me in my career that did not, and still had not, advanced my career. I was angry and sad, sitting in disbelief and generally feeling all the feelings. I was even more taken aback to realize that I had not seen this tendency before. I had been duped! How could I have not seen this? Here I was, advocating for women's rights, and suddenly realized I was put on a sideways path to nowhere. I am still appalled and stunned when I think about it.

In my role, I had stepped up and led, but because it was volunteer-related work, it was not impacting the bottom line and therefore did not count. I could break into the club to get on those high-visibility projects that would have the potential to move my career forward. I had blinders on, and I conducted my projects for which I was responsible to the best of my ability and was told as much. I even asked for more work and delivered twice as much as others on the team. Did that make an impact on my bonus? No, it did not. When Covid came around and the workload increased, I volunteered even more. In some cases, I was "voluntold" to lead the task-related work. Did it impact my career? No.

The reason for pointing this out is because I believe it is fundamentally important to share with you, my dear reader, how to look at what you want in your career and in life and not make the same mistake I did. Realize which tasks lead to nowhere. Look for opportunities that will advance your career and decline those tasks that do not.

The bottom line is that we place our own chains on ourselves. We stay inside the cage that society has placed us in. Too often, we stay small, and we don't self-advocate. We think if we just work harder, then we will be rewarded in this life. Well, if we are only making 82 cents on the dollar or less than what men are earning for the same job, no matter how many hours, going the extra mile, or taking on more responsibility without the pay, we will never be equals. It is a system that is NOT designed in our favor and is even worse for women of color. We MUST be the change we want to see in the world and not give up. Stop trying to find meaning in a construct designed to limit you.

---

1. Inc.com, "The Elephant and the Rope: One Mental Trick to Unlock Your Growth," https://www.inc.com/ryan-holmes/the-elephant-and-the-rope-one-mental-trick-to-unlock-your-growth.html
2. McKinsey.com, "Women in the Workplace 2021," https://www.mckinsey.com/featured-insights/diversity-and-inclusion/women-in-the-workplace#

CHAPTER 5
NOT KNOWING

How is it possible to know what we want if we have been conditioned to think of possibilities from the constraints of being inside the box?

Plato's allegory of the cave is a perfect model to use to help explain this concept more fully. In Plato's book, *The Republic*, he describes prisoners chained in a cave, forced to face the back wall of the cave. There is a fire burning behind these men. People described as puppeteers hold puppets in front of the fire in such a way as to cast shadows onto the back of the cave wall for these chained prisoners to see. These prisoners believe the puppets and sounds they hear are real, and they try to figure out the meaning. At one point, one of the prisoners breaks his chains and leaves the cave. He discovers that the shadows on the wall that he thought were real were not. In fact, it was these puppeteers who were purposefully casting these shadows. He tries to tell the other prisoners about the puppets, but they don't believe him.

There are comparisons between this allegory and our world today where people are focused heavily on social media and think the lives portrayed therein are real. We are conditioned by all the societal norms discussed earlier in this book and cannot see what is actually taking place. As women, we have been raised to think differently. In addition, societal expectations of how we should act because we are women help to enforce the narrative. As a result, we do not truly know ourselves and rarely question what we were taught.

We do not know ourselves because:

1. We never question our motives. Never do we question why we chose the friends, the partner, the job, and the life we have. Why is that the case? There are times when I have questioned friends that I had at various times in my life and thought about their life choices that seemed detrimental. In some cases, I distanced myself from them because I wanted something different and wanted to be around others who felt similarly. In those cases, it was quite clear to me that I made a positive choice for my long-term goals.

But what about my husband? I chose him because he was authoritarian, like my father. I unconsciously chose that type of personality because it was familiar. It was only later that I realized what I had done and why. Needless to say, we divorced.

Many times, we think we have thought about our decisions when, in truth, these decisions are usually from the perspective of our operating system developed early in life. These installed beliefs are ones that we never stopped to think about or examine. If we grew up with a deep sense of not being valued or worthy, how would we know to pick a partner who treats us with respect? How could we get a job where we could truly be ourselves and live up to our full potential? It is impossible because we never questioned our intentions. Most likely, we never even knew to set intentions. We reason out things by saying, "This job pays enough money for me to have a nice living, so I will stay here and not rock the boat," while mistakenly believing this is all you deserve in life. Or we might say, "My partner's behavior is demeaning at times, but he provides for our family," choosing to stay and allow that behavior to continue. Ultimately, the end result is that you compromise your life. This pattern of behavior is soul-crushing over time and leads to unhappiness. You can learn to change your behavior and not accept demeaning remarks rather than simply accepting your lot in life.

2. The way we view ourselves is distorted, and we don't even realize it. It is very challenging to see ourselves. Often, we lean on others to tell us their view of what they see in us. The problem is that we tend to not believe their view a lot of the time. It is like being inside a glass jar and trying to read the outside label. You can't do it from the inside. Then, when others describe us, we generally don't accept the positive things our friend might say, but we certainly are willing to embrace the negative perspectives. When we have a negative view of ourselves and believe that to be true, we filter out things that do not fit with our beliefs. This phenomenon is one of many reasons we have a distorted view of ourselves.

3. However, if you think about how women are conditioned in society to think, act, and look, how could we have a true perception of who we are? Have you ever questioned why you wear makeup? Why don't most men feel the need to cover their blemishes with foundation? (At this time, men are starting to wear makeup, but it is not as predominantly accepted as it is for women to do so.) This societal conditioning keeps us feeling less than others. These behaviors are fundamental parts of our lives that we just do rather than stop to think about their reasons. How can we truly know ourselves if we do not question everything and determine our own course of action based on what we want to become?

•   •   •

4. We don't even know our own needs and expect a partner to fulfill them for us instead of fulfilling our own needs first. According to a *Huffington Post* article, as women, we have a long generational history where we have been intentionally hushed and had our needs suppressed by the patriarchy and sexism. [1]

Some women grew up with the belief that everyone else's needs should come first. If these women did attempt to put their own needs first, they were ostracized or made to feel bad for doing so. While my mom did not say to me to place others' needs ahead of my own, I watched her do it, and I modeled my behaviors after hers. At times in my life, I have also put others' needs ahead of my own in relationships. I have witnessed other women in my family and friends doing the same thing. By placing others' needs first, we never stop to think about our own needs. If this is the case, how can women who have learned to accept this belief ever discover their own needs? Chances are, they won't. Then, when entering a relationship with a partner, these women do everything they can to make their partners happy, even at their own expense. For example, they might allow their dates to choose the activities they will do on a date, watch the movies their partner always picks, and go to the restaurants their partners want to frequent.

Later in the relationship, if women start wanting to change and speak up or advocate for the things they would prefer to do, their partners might be surprised and wonder what happened to the person who liked the same things they liked. In these circumstances, women might continue to advocate for what they want, but in other situations, they might fear losing their partner, so they continue to push down their needs for the sake of staying together. This is just one example of how putting others' needs ahead of our own causes us to be out of touch with ourselves and not develop our own needs.

This phenomenon can also show up in the workplace. For example, you might be asked to take on tasks that are not in your job description, like getting coffee for the boss, arranging luncheons, or other tasks that no one else is asked to perform, even if they are your peers. Putting others' needs ahead of our own also shows up in our lives as settling for jobs and not trying to negotiate for a higher salary. If you have researched and discovered that most others in your same position have a higher salary, you are well within your right to ask for more. The trouble is that most women do not ask because of our social conditioning. Whether in our personal or professional lives, putting others' needs ahead of our own can prevent us from learning what our own needs are. This behavior prevents us from finding the relationships or jobs that enable us to meet our needs, which ultimately could give us a more fulfilling life.

5. We never develop our own sense of self. Instead, we create a false sense of self to fit in with others. Have you met people who attend church because it is part of their societal structure instead of attending because of the deep sense of meaning it provides? Or have you ever found yourself doing something because you are "supposed to" even though you do not enjoy it? Have you ever gone along with a joke and laughed even though you knew it was derogatory and did not believe it to be funny? Most of us have found ourselves in those situations at times. When you live your entire life that way, surrounded by people who think that it is ok to be offensive or rude to others, it is akin to wearing a mask over your face, always hiding who you truly are. It is a fake existence that wears a person down over time.

Many people never think about living their own lives on their own terms and pretend to like other people when they do not. An example of this type of behavior is pretending we like our lives when we have a deep feeling of unhappiness. We tell ourselves it is fine, just like a well-meaning parent who tells you everything is ok and to stop crying.

Consider people in unhappy marriages who stay in them because it is easier to do so than summoning the courage it would take to leave. People who leave miserable relationships often remark on how much happier they are after leaving and could not understand why it took them so long to make that decision. That is an example of pretending. It is hard to do the things necessary to make lasting change, to look deeply within ourselves, and do the difficult things needed in order to move forward and grow. That is the bottom line, however—to find our sense of self, it requires us to change. We fear change because we know what it is like to live the way we are living right now. It takes a lot of courage, guts, and stamina to change. That is the reason most people do not do anything and continue to live their lives pretending they are happy.

Now that we understand a few reasons why we do not know ourselves, let's look at a few areas where not knowing ourselves causes problems for us in life.

6. We go after jobs/careers for the wrong reasons. Most people start out going after jobs that provide the most income. That makes sense because we need money in order to live independently, and it is important to be able to pay for rent, food, utilities, and a car. Beyond that, many do not give much thought to what type of career they want. While there are some folks who know what they want to do and go after those goals, a majority of us do not know what we want to do with our lives or what job would provide the most satisfaction or meaning. Instead, we get comfortable and hopefully climb the corporate ladder somewhat. But over time, we gain a sense of unease and unhappiness, feeling that there should be more to this life than simply going to work, taking care of the family, going to bed, and doing it over again every day.

While there is more to life than the daily grind, how many of us never take the time to figure it out? We do not reflect on our lives and those things that would help us feel more fulfilled. So instead, we tell ourselves, "My life is good. I have a good job, a nice house, a stable partner, and I am happy enough."

Over time, you become increasingly unhappy and cannot put your finger on the exact reasons why. Part of the reason is that we have never taken the time to learn about our own needs, about ourselves in general, and we don't understand at a deep level the reasons for our motivations or learn why we act the way we do. Then, we go out and get jobs once again without understanding ourselves and our motivations. This is the situation most of us find ourselves in, and having a job for the wrong reasons leads to unhappiness.

Feeling unfulfilled in our careers and constantly wishing for something better or continually job-shopping perpetuates the external nature of how we decide to seek answers. By not knowing ourselves and seeking answers externally, this behavior further keeps us from knowing ourselves. We must learn and know who we are in order to have a job and a life in which we feel satisfied. Getting a promotion, a new job, and a higher salary can be unrewarding in the long-term if we are seeking those things for the wrong reasons.

7. We aren't ambitious enough, or we are too ambitious to the detriment of relationships and ourselves. When we do not know ourselves, we tend to limit our ambitions or have unrealistic expectations about what we can achieve. Once we try and fail, many of us don't try again. When our entire lives are based on societal norms that we have never questioned and simply have accepted, we limit ourselves in terms of what is possible. There-fore, we do not aspire to our full potential.

. . .

8. Our definitions of success are often not ones we set for ourselves. Success is largely determined by social media, our families' view of what it means to be successful, and our friends and colleagues. We might think it is our own definition of success because it fits into a societally accepted description, but it is not one we created and therefore feels meaningless when we achieve it. In addition, we might feel self-doubt, thinking that we didn't really earn success or that it was not that big of a deal after all. Or we are not willing to change and learn the things we would need to develop if we were to move into something bigger. We keep the chains on ourselves and don't even realize it. We have the ability to unlock and remove the chains that bind us in most circumstances, but we are afraid to do the things it requires of us to make those changes. Therefore, we stay small. We don't go for that better job; we tell ourselves we are happy and content where we are when the truth is that we are not willing to make the changes, and it is better and easier to stay content rather than to try to take on that seemingly more difficult job. It might only be difficult at first; just like any change, there is a period of uncertainty as you learn the ropes, but many are afraid even to try.

9. We remain stuck. Feeling stuck is generally the feeling we get when we are in a relationship that feels unfulfilling (maybe we know we should leave but decide to stay because it is safe). The same could be said about our friendships—have we chosen people, or have they chosen us? Do those friendships also feel unfulfilling, or do they energize you? If we do not attempt something better in our lives, we will remain stuck in place. We become stagnant, and that leads to feeling bad in general. For many, it leads to depression. It is hard to make decisions or even set goals because you do not really know what you want. Maybe you never sat down and figured out what you wanted for your life or even

tried to understand yourself more fully. Feeling stuck has a lot to do with not exploring who you are and what you want out of life.

Does this sound like you?

When we do not understand the game that is being played, it causes misunderstandings that lead to unhappy lives. It is important to understand the landscape and where you fit into it. Once those aspects are understood, the new rules I am about to share with you can be applied, and you will create your own strategy to move forward. But first, one more very large problem occurs from not understanding the game, which is self-doubt.

---

1. Huffpost.com, "Why Do Women Find It So Hard to Put Themselves First?" https://www.huffpost.com/entry/why-do-women-find-it-so-d_b_7621976

CHAPTER 6
SELF-DOUBT (IMPOSTER SYNDROME)

While it is currently a popular expression, there is some debate on the definition of the term "imposter syndrome." An article where this syndrome was first mentioned states, "First described by psychologists Suzanne Imes, PhD, and Pauline Rose Clance, PhD, in the 1970s, impostor phenomenon occurs among high achievers who are unable to internalize and accept their success. They often attribute their accomplishments to luck rather than to ability, and fear that others will eventually unmask them as a fraud."[1]

Another article shares more insight into the definition of this phenomena, "… doubting your abilities and feeling like a fraud at work, is a diagnosis often given to women. But the fact that it's considered a diagnosis at all is problematic. The concept, whose development in the 70s excluded the effects of systemic racism, classism, xenophobia, and other biases, took a fairly universal feeling of discomfort, second-guessing, and mild anxiety in the workplace and pathologized it, especially for women. The answer to overcoming imposter syndrome is not to fix individuals, but to create an environment that fosters a number of different leadership styles and where diversity of racial, ethnic, and gender identities is viewed as just as professional as the current model."[2]

While the term is still being defined, it is essential to note that women might be subject to psychiatric gaslighting. Manipulating someone by psychological means that results in them questioning their sanity is gaslighting. Most people, in general, have self-doubt, but when it comes to a diagnosis, imposter syndrome is not yet a medical diagnosis. The majority of the people identified with having Imposter Syndrome are women. Is this a genuinely disproportionate medical diagnosis?

There can be several reasons for this phenomenon, such as women trying to perform and showcase their talents in a male-dominated world and still not being recognized for their work itself. This topic can be an entire book on its own, so I will not delve further on the subject.

The definition to which I am referring is more along the lines of not feeling worthy of having the job you currently have or not feeling good enough for the salary you are given. Therefore, you might work extra hard to prove your value. I am not referring to the systemic discrimination that exists in many corporate cultures where women are not made to feel welcome to begin with, especially women of color. There are additional biases that exist in the workplace, especially for women of color. An article titled "The Concrete Ceiling" explains that women of color are overlooked for promotions in a disproportionate number. The article goes on to say, "For years, companies have framed diversity in tech as a 'pipeline' problem—that the reason for the lack of diversity is due to there not being enough qualified talent from different backgrounds. This claim is not only untrue but also dismisses the effects of racism on people's careers."[3]

In those cases, women have to prove over and over again that they deserve to be there, but despite their achievements, others do not accept them. That phenomenon, unfortunately, exists as well. When discrimination occurs, we must demand a better and more inclusive culture from leadership. For this reason, many women start their own businesses rather than tolerate the micro-aggressions and outright discrimination they have faced.

The self-doubt upon which I want to focus is innate in all of us, especially women who are attempting to fit into a culture that is dictating how they should behave. How many of you have gotten to a certain level and looked over your shoulder thinking, *Someone is going to figure out that I don't deserve to be here, I'm not good enough,* or had similar thoughts flowing through your mind?

I have, and I know most of us feel that way too. When I coach people, this is the number one thing that I see time and time again. Too often, women doubt themselves and do not feel worthy of their achievements. This can be due to many things, but a sense of unworthiness is the primary driver for all variations.

Feeling unworthy happens to all people, men included. I would say that more women experience this feeling of not being good enough or are afraid to aspire for more in their careers more so than men do. I base that on a few studies, one of which was conducted by Hewlett-Packard, where they found that men applied for a job when they met only 60 percent of the qualifications, but women applied only if they met 100 percent of them.

At LinkedIn, the world's largest professional network on the internet, they too captured data that indicates a similar phenomenon. "Women tend to screen themselves out of the conversation and end up applying to fewer jobs than men," authors Deanne Tockey and Maria Ignatova wrote. The bottom line is that even though both men and women were similarly interested in new jobs, compared to men, women applied to 20 percent fewer jobs and were 16 percent less likely to apply after viewing a job.

This research indicates that women feel insecure about themselves and feel the need to possess the exact skills before they apply for a job. Women tend to feel less competent than men, even if we have several degrees and certifications. You might feel self-doubt and then go into overdrive and overachieve to prove your worth. You might even go as far as attributing your success to luck or other factors, never allowing your actual accomplishments to be recognized by yourself. There are many cases where a woman is recognized by someone, but she does not truly believe that she deserves the praise or shrugs it off as she tells herself, "It's not a big deal." It is a big deal, and we should acknowledge and celebrate our achievements.

Why don't we?

Self-doubt plays a huge role in our lives, and it is extremely important to be aware of where and how it is holding you back so that you can master the Game of Life!

I once coached a woman who felt like she didn't have the right to be where she was in her role. When I was coaching her, I discovered while she had received positive feedback from her peers and her manager, she focused on the one item her manager said she could improve upon. The item was trivial. Nonetheless, she focused entirely on that one piece of feedback to her own detriment. She felt that because this one item was mentioned, all her other acknowledged accomplishments were worthless.

Think about this for a moment. When someone says, "You really have done a great job on this project," do you immediately say, "It was a team effort." You might be telling yourself, "I don't do that," or "I have never done that before." But then I would ask you, have you ever deflected a compliment? When someone says to you "You look great," do you say something like, "Oh I overslept and didn't have time to wash my hair," instead of saying "Thank you?"

Think about a time when someone paid you a compliment about your hair after you woke up that morning and spent over an hour trying to calm it down or make it look somewhat presentable, or when you bought that new blouse but decided the color wasn't really that flattering. At work, when someone says, "What a pretty blouse!" you quickly blurt out, "Yeah, I bought it online and am not a fan of this color on me," rather than simply thanking the person who noticed.

Why do we do that?

It turns out that the human brain is primed to look for threats in our environment. In fact, it is called "negativity bias," where we remember and even dwell on the negative things that happen to us much more so than the positive events. For an example of this, I recommend trying a little experiment: think about your past week and things that happened at work. For most people, all the negative events come to mind first. Then, when trying very hard, we can remember some positive things that happened as well. Usually, those positive events are lost from memory because they are dominated by negativity bias. A great article explaining this in more detail can be found here: https://www.verywellmind.com/negative-bias-4589618.[4] Turns out, we are wired that way because being aware of threats has helped us survive in the distant past when a tiger might have been chasing us or about to pounce on our children. Over time, this has resulted in a focus on negative things more so than positive. This constant scanning for threats affects both men and women. Add to that the fact that these perceived problems do not always reflect reality. If we believe that we are undeserving, we cannot accept any praise for a job well done because we likely won't believe it.

Going back to the blouse scenario, we believe the blouse to be unflattering. Therefore, if anyone wants to pay us a compliment, we don't believe it is true and deflect or discount any praise someone might offer.

The same phenomenon happens in our careers. When we doubt ourselves and our capabilities, no matter how much we have accomplished, we focus only on those things we did wrong instead of the various things we did right that got us to where we are today.

When you add self-doubt and not knowing yourself deeply, these issues lead to a deeper sense of insecurity. You might need extra reassurance because you feel anxious. Worse, you might get to a point where you do not make any decisions related to your job because you are stuck in terms of what you want to do in your career instead of allowing the normal function of general self-doubt to propel us to do something different in our lives, in many cases, self-doubt leads to paralysis.

Not knowing ourselves creates confusing and unfulfilled lives. We know we should feel good about our lives, but we just don't and cannot quite put our finger on our reasons for feeling uncertain. Now, you know the simple truth—you must know the game you are playing.

Does any of this sound like you?

- Do you spend hours worrying about a misstep at work that you took responsibility for (even if it was not your fault)?
- Do you always think that you got where you are due to luck or simply being in the right place at the right time?
- Are you always seeking others' feedback because you feel insecure about something? Do you believe getting someone's praise will bolster your feelings of worthiness?
- Do you feel like a phony, as if you do not really know what's going on and you are just trying to keep up?

If any of those things sound like you, keep reading. For those of you who might be new to this topic, you might be reeling from all this information presented. Take heart! There is good news!

You can make a difference. The first step is knowledge, then awareness.

The next section of this book will help you to better understand yourself so you can figure out what you want to do next in your life and help you create your own rules so you succeed in your personal Game of Life!

---

1. American Psychological Association, "Feel Like a Fraud?" https://www.apa.org/gradpsych/2013/11/fraud
2. Harvard Business Review, "Stop Telling Women They Have Imposter Syndrome," https://hbr.org/2021/02/stop-telling-women-they-have-imposter-syndrome
3. Stanford Social Innovation Review, "The Concrete Ceiling," https://ssir.org/articles/entry/the_concrete_ceiling
4. VeryWellMind, "What is the Negativity Bias?" https://www.verywellmind.com/negative-bias-4589618.

SECTION III: THE NEW RULES

HOW TO PLAY THE GAME OF LIFE

CHAPTER 7
CREATING A VISION FOR YOUR LIFE

I have spent many years in the technology space, working in IT. Information technology (IT) uses computers, software, and much more to ensure electronic data works as expected within business operations. For example, the data captured about you when hired into an organization is also used to ensure your paycheck is accurate.

As the software world has evolved, there are now entire software solutions you can just buy and use in the cloud. "The cloud" is what we call servers that are accessed over the Internet and the software and databases that run on those servers. Cloud servers are located in data centers all over the world. What this means is that instead of a company having to invest in storing, managing, and updating servers in server rooms, they simply access servers from companies that have already done that in data centers. Further, companies want to focus on running their businesses and would rather buy software from a cloud provider instead of attempting to build it themselves. Because this appears to be so easy to do, many businesses buy cloud software in the hopes that it will solve their business problems. Still, there is a lot of work involved to ensure the new software works properly. There are integrations between current systems and the new system. How do we set these things up to make it easy for our employees to use? As the project manager, I manage the work that is being done to make those things happen.

One of the many fundamental reasons why I see projects fail has to do with people not clearly addressing the reason for purchasing the new software. It is crucial when making a purchase to ask, "Does the software align with the corporate vision/mission/corporate goals?" If the answer is "yes" to that question, then there need to be answers to these questions: Why do we need it? What will it do? How will it help?

What generally happens is someone sees a new piece of software they believe will make things better. The vendor sells that person on all the bells and whistles and things that the software can do. That person gets excited and tells the company IT leaders, "We must have that shiny new thing!" Then, IT installs it. But it turns out the shiny new thing does not always help. "Why?" you might ask. One might say, "It didn't work because no one sat down and looked at all the business processes and tools already in place; no one did the work to figure out how or why this tool was going to help."

Or, in explaining why an expensive new shiny object doesn't work, someone might offer this explanation: "It was poorly planned, and all the steps taken did not lead to the right outcome as a result." Yes, that is a strong answer as well.

But what about asking, "Why?" Why not ask why we need a new shiny tool? Does it fit in with my corporate vision/mission/strategy/goals? If so, how? If not, why would we have gotten approval to move forward with it?

Let us bring that back to my life. When I began working as a project manager, did I know my corporate vision/mission/goals? Was I familiar with my north star, otherwise known as my reason for being on this planet? I must confess that I did not. It wasn't due to a lack of planning. On the contrary, I had been making plans and getting things done all my life.

What was missing was my overarching vision in life. I did not take the time to invest in myself and figure out what I wanted to achieve in my lifetime. Without this reflection, how would the goals I set for myself be tied to what I wanted to accomplish? Further, how would I even know if I was successful?

I realize this is difficult for most people. If your life up to present has been filled with the idea that you should not worry about getting ahead, that you should get married and have children, and that domestic life would be your job, then that vision for your life was already created for you—but not necessarily by you.

This is an important concept to grasp.

I will say it again: we do not sit down and take the time to truly figure out what we want to do in our lives because society, movies, and books already tell us the vision. We hear, "Go to college, get a job, have a family, retire."

When you were a child, did you dream of being in the job you hold today? Where did your dreams go? A teacher may have told you that the chances of being a famous singer, actress, etc., were very slim. Instead, they encouraged you to get a degree and a good-paying job and said, "Don't waste your time." So, we stopped dreaming and followed their direction. In some cases, we are too ingrained in our societal roles as women, and we do not even dream of something bigger for ourselves. We meet the boy/girl and get married, and our dreams go right out the window. We go through life thinking this is what we are supposed to do, but many of us end up feeling hollow, and unfulfilled.

Many women come to my coaching practice because they feel stuck in their lives. Is it any wonder why? Between society, parents, teachers, limited career advancement opportunities, and salary that is less than we deserve, we learn to stay small. It is up to us to break these chains that bind us and find meaning in our lives. The first step toward that goal is to take the time and think about what you want the rest of your life to mean to you.

In order to break the chains that bind you, you must be aware of the landscape and how you arrived at where you are today. What is the next step?

The First Rule: Create a Vision for Your Life

It is your one and only life. And you are in the driver's seat, which means YOU are responsible for creating a vision for your life. The good news is that it does not matter if you are eighteen or eighty. It is never too late to start.

This action is a big one and is the most important step you can take. This vision you create for yourself should not be made from that place within a box (the one society/parents/friends placed on you) but one from a limitless perspective. The best way to get started is to think about how you feel. How do you feel about doing the same job you are in now for the rest of your life? Would that bring you joy? If not, what would? Let the thoughts come out. Write them down on paper. It is ok to be bold. Go for it! Write as many examples as you can. There is a practice of journaling where you ask a question, set a time, and write as much as you can the answers to that question. Keep doing this until you come up with a theme for what it is you want. I will discuss more in-depth information about journaling in Chapter 11. For now, continue writing your answers to questions like:

- What are my hopes and dreams?
- What were my dreams when I was a child, a teenager?
- How are my dreams now different from when I was a child or teenager?
- What else do I want to do with my life?

Taking time to write out the answers to these questions will help you create a vision for your life. Don't play small. Think big!

Let's review the definitions of the terms I am using.

- **Mission** = What you aspire to be in life. It can be referred to as your "dream" for your life, even your "soul's purpose." Let's use an example similar to my personal mission: "I want to help people find their life's purpose and help them create goals to ensure they reach their vision for their life."
- **Vision** = a general statement of how you will achieve your mission. Mine is "I will help people reach their life's goals by writing books, creating a planner, having them attend my courses, and 1-1 coaching where they can jump-start their lives."
- **Goals** = are things you need to measure to ensure the successful implementation of your vision. Sample goals might be to write a book by XYZ date, start offering the courses by ABC date, etc.

Many well-meaning people create goals to achieve in their lives without sitting down first to create a mission. They might accomplish these goals and still feel empty. The reason is that these goals were not made after first defining a mission for themselves. If I am making goals that are not founded on my vision, then I am simply making tactical decisions and not reaching my full potential. Therefore, it is extremely important to take the time, invest in yourself, and figure out your mission for your life. I believe it is one of the most fundamentally important exercises we as humans can embark upon.

A mission will help give you meaning in your life. The vision gives you direction on what to do and where to go, knowing what jobs to go for next and why you want them. Without this vision, we end up in the next job without really having a clear under-standing of why we want that role or if it will lead to something better. It's like being on a ship without a rudder—in other words, directionless. You end up being pushed along the current and the waves versus knowing exactly where you are going and the reasons why you are headed there. Big difference!

Let's use a few real examples of mission and vision statements from companies you might know:

Company: Tesla
Mission: To accelerate the world's transition to sustainable energy.
Vision: To create the most compelling car company of the 21st century by driving the world's transition to electric vehicles.[1]

Company: Meta (formerly known as Facebook)
Mission: To give people the power to build community and bring the world closer together.
Vision: People use Facebook to stay connected with friends and family, to discover what's going on in the world, and to share and express what matters to them.[2]

Defining your mission and vision is an instrumental way to help you plan and reach your goals. Below is an example of how I have defined my own.

Several of my key strengths include learning, strategy, and planning. I have been on a lifelong mission to figure out my mission! Better yet, because I am great at and love learning, I researched the works of several experts in this field, synthesized their teachings, and distilled things down to a simple system. This system helps a person focus on the right questions to ask and helps them incorporate those answers into a daily practice that begins them on the journey of self-discovery in a way like no other program I have found. A few of the books I recommend out of the many I've read include *The Success Principles* by Jack Canfield, *The Seven Habits of Highly Effective People* by Steven R. Covey, and *How to Win Friends and Influence People* by Dale Carnegie. I have incorporated their key learnings and added elements that helped me. I have shared this approach with friends and family, and they have benefitted tremendously.

Because I want to share what I have learned with other people, I determined my mission is to "Help people live their best lives." Then, I defined my vision which is to "Use my book, courses, and coaching to give people a framework to help them achieve the life they desire."

When I look at all of the possible career choices that I might want to attain, I narrow it down to the ones that align with my mission and vision. That helps me stay on track and brings more focus into my life. Sure, I can learn how to become an accountant and help maintain the financial aspects of a business, but is that profession in alignment with my mission and vision? One could argue that it might help people to live their best lives because now that they are freed up from accounting tasks and responsibilities, they can focus on living their best lives. However, it doesn't teach them how to do so.

Determining my strengths and weaknesses also helps me to better understand those aspects of potential roles I may be considering to see if the strengths I possess align with the strengths the role requires. If a potential role aligns more with the items that are in my weakest areas instead of my strongest areas, I would not likely be happy in that role until I built up those weaker areas. The work would always be a struggle until I developed the skills needed and mastered them.

We find more meaning in our lives when we face and overcome challenges. When we become content in life, it is great for a while, but then we start to notice that things are boring and begin to feel unhappy. It is when you are in that space of unhappiness that we have an opportunity to think about what we want to do next. Sometimes, the next thing we consider is too big or scary, and we talk ourselves out of going for it. The problem then becomes a life not lived versus a life lived. Taking the time to figure out your mission helps to anchor what you want to achieve in your life and the reasons why you want to achieve them. It becomes your north star. Then, when you start achieving your goals, you might find you need to update your mission and vision because you've learned new things and now you have a new understanding of what you want in your life. That is perfectly normal and means you are growing! Growing and learning are keys to a well lived life. The more you learn, grow, and achieve, the more meaningful your life becomes.

Okay, now let's discuss the dark side. What happens when we fall off track?

I am not perfect at this process of always making sure I am staying true to my mission or updating my vision, and I get stuck along the way at times. It is hard. It is difficult to stay on track with your life in relation to your mission. Many people know what they are "supposed" to do, and we do it for a while, but then we fall off-track. Sometimes we get back on track with our mission and go forward but later fall off-track again. Why is that?

We fall off-track because we are human! We see a new job, company, or opportunity, and we go for it because someone tells us we'd be good at it. We might hear that the new job is paying more money or some other reason that deviates us from our path. We do not take the time to first determine if it fits into what we said we wanted—our mission and vision. If we desert our current path for a title change but no real opportunity for upward growth, we will find ourselves stuck in the same place, just a sliver higher than we were before but even more stuck in a role that will not lead to what we envisioned for ourselves. Therefore, having your mission in front of you every day helps you to make better decisions about where it is you wish to land in your next role and why you want to do it in the first place. It acts as your north star, so you have a better chance of remaining on your path.

There is another aspect to this as well. Sometimes, we self-sabotage our own mission and vision with self-doubt. I want to be the first to admit to you that staying true to your mission and vision is not all roses and sunshine. I am a glass-half-full person, and I am always looking for the positive. If I wrote this book with only a positive outlook, then I would be missing half the story. I would not be revealing the full truth—the dark side we all have inside of us. I am referring to the self-doubts, the fear we might not want to feel, the voices in our heads that say, "You can't do that," and all the negative beliefs that stand in our way to self-improvement. I could not imagine how sharing only the happy side of the process would help anyone. I know that it would not.

I intend to keep it real. Because I want everyone to know that this glass-is-half-full gal has demons and a dark side. If anyone denies that they have dark days or brushes it off as not a big deal, they are missing out on a full, beautiful, meaningful life.

For example, maybe you know that your next step is to move into a role where you must speak in front of audiences several times a month, but you have a tremendous fear of public speaking. You know that everything that you have learned, achieved, and done has led you to this point in time, and that this role is the perfect position to move you ahead on your mission. But you have this fear of public speaking. What do you do? Stay stuck in fear and pass on the role? If you choose the path of not accepting the role, you are deciding to let fear dictate your life. Do you think you would truly be satisfied with your life if you deviated from the path you wanted?

When we take the easy path, we feel comfortable and safe at the time, but it starts to eat away at us. We become unhappy over time. We always wonder what if we did take the role and did something to overcome the fear of public speaking? What would our life have been like? People living in safety and not taking risks are dreamers, not action-takers. Sure, new challenges are difficult and could be risky, but staying in place is not always the right choice. In the article "Not Taking Risks is the Riskiest Career Move of All" by Anne Kreamer, published in *Harvard Business Review*, Kreamer says that we are "…wired to resist giving up the known for the unknown." [3]

What if instead of staying in your old job, you worked with a coach to help you overcome your fear of public speaking, or joined Toastmasters (a club dedicated to helping people excel in public speaking and overcoming fears through practice)? Another technique that may help is to journal about your feelings, thoughts, and things happening in your life. I get into more depth about the importance of journaling and how it helps in Chapter 11. With a plan like that in place, you would have a greater chance of overcoming your fear instead of a lifetime of wondering, *What if…?*

When we take on those difficult challenges and fail, we can try and try again until we succeed. Albert Einstein said, "A person who never made a mistake never tried anything."

For those dark days where even small challenges seem overwhelming, it is helpful to remember that this will pass.

Just as there is a dark side to life, there is also beauty.

Life is beautiful. As I look out of my window, (I sometimes have to keep curtains drawn or my 160-pound beast of a dog will start barking at squirrels or other dogs walking by) I notice the trees outside. Spring has sprung and newly formed vibrant green leaves now cover the branches making everything brighter. Nonetheless, life is BEAUTIFUL. In all its glory, with the trees, the light, the clouds, the sky, the wind, and the sounds. I soak it in and enjoy it so much.

Though it sounds contradictory, beauty can be found even in our darkest times. To be clear, I do not advocate for acts of violence, aggression, or intentional (or unintentional) harm to others. That is not what I mean.

Pain and suffering are beautiful, too. To be clear, I do not advocate for acts of violence, aggression, or intentional (or unintentional) harm to others. That is not what I mean. Never should any of that be deliberately caused or perpetrated on anyone. There is no beauty in any violent, against-the-universe act against another sentient being. Ever. Period. Let me better explain by giving a personal example.

When my mother passed away, I was there holding her hand. My sister and stepfather were there as well. We were by her side for the previous thirty days as she lay in bed in hospice. It was so hard. There was so much to say, and she had dementia, so who knew if it was getting through. Crying, regret, overwhelming grief, tears, depression, so many aspects of grief were displayed. Yet, in the midst, there were acts of kindness shown to us by the staff. They demonstrated respect for our grief and suffering. The love and care we shared with our mom, wife, and grandmother was beautiful. So, when I remember the pain of her passing, and I also remember the beauty.

I cannot pretend to know what it might have been like for someone who has had severe traumatic experiences. What I will say is that you still have your life. It is yours. Your life belongs to you. You get to choose how you will move on from here. YOU get to choose! That is beautiful. Despite what happened before, YOU have the opportunity to put yourself in the driver's seat of YOUR life. The person you are, that you will be, that YOU get to decide you will be, is the most beautiful gift.

Daily Decisions

Each and every day, we have decisions to make. Micro (deciding not to eat that junk food in the evenings) or macro (should I take that new job?), they all add up to one thing: am I living my life in alignment with my vision? Your daily actions will tell you if you are on track or not. Therefore, reflecting on your daily activities and decisions will help you to remain in alignment with your mission.

Getting clear involves thoughtful daily decisions. That new day, today, is what you get to create, no matter what happened yesterday, a year ago, or a minute ago. Who will you choose to be right now? This choice, it turns out, is a daily decision. Let us say you decide to give up smoking, cursing, drinking, sugar, or something else. Day one is great. You are on track; things are going well. Day two is a little more difficult. You have the urge to have that cigarette or eat that candy because it is your ritual; it is your go-to habit. It is a decision to go one way or the other. Sometimes we go for the thing on autopilot, and it is done before we have consciously realized, *Oh, wait, I said I wasn't going to do this anymore.* But it happened. Now what? For me, I have said to myself in the past, *okay, well, it is a rough day; I am going to have that piece of candy; I deserve it.* Then, I stop thinking about deciding to eat the candy. Decision-making is hard. It requires thought, attention, reminders, and strength to stick it out once you say "no" to the thing you wanted to stop doing. No wonder we so often fall off the wagon when attempting to act on our plans.

But you get to choose to get back up. That is strength. That is determination and grit. Getting back up is crucial. And it is the hardest thing to do. I know. I fall down a lot! But I get back up because I am learning, and I am choosing to get back up and move forward. Whether it is micro-steps or baby-steps, all the steps move us forward.

When you notice negative patterns of behavior, check them against your mission. For example, if I said my vision is that I want to help people live their best lives, yet I am eating two boxes of chocolate every night in an attempt to self-soothe and not face the feelings that are trying to surface, then how can I coach others to live their best lives if I am not facing my own? If I am not taking care of myself, there is a risk I won't be healthy enough to help anyone. I realize this is a very simplistic example, but the point is that having your mission identified and clear helps you to stay on track in many aspects of your life.

That brings me to discipline. I love to hate this word. I know I need discipline to make the choice every day to get back up and keep fighting the good fight. We will discuss this more in Chapter 12 – Discipline: The World's Greatest Drug.

But I am only fooling myself. The struggle is REAL!

That is why we need to figure out this discipline thing to be successful. It is also why I chose that title for the chapter and refer to discipline as a drug. You will learn more about that in the upcoming chapter. I hope this introduction to the concept intrigues you enough to keep reading. The point is, I respect the struggle. It is exceedingly difficult to maintain. If we support the attitude that we recognize the struggle is real, we keep it real and keep moving forward. I always think of Dory (played by Ellen DeGeneres) from the movie *Finding Nemo,* "Just keep swimming." Take that first step. Keep moving forward. Life is beautiful. Rejoice in your first step. You took the step. That is beautiful.

This system is helping me. I have researched self-help gurus, planners, books, videos, and more. Some things were missing. Mainly for me, what was missing is my "why." Why am I doing this thing or that thing? What is it that I want for my life? Who do I want to be?

That "why" is what I was missing and what I learned how to get closer to. None of these things are new but are simply repackaged in an honest, open, real dialogue in the hopes that it will help you, too.

Here are some examples of others this system has helped:

One friend, an artist, has had an idea for a piece of artwork that she has been sitting on for over four years. She knows how to make it happen, she understands the way she will sell it once it is created, but she has not moved it forward. Using my system, she is now selling her artwork, understands what was blocking her from moving forward, and has overcome the challenges because she now has more clarity.

Another success story with using my system is a small business owner who knew there was more to her life than running her business. She was successful but still felt empty inside. Implementing my system helped her gain clarity around a new, complementary business that is helping others on a level she had never envisioned before. And she found her true purpose, her true north star in the process.

This system works. It worked for me and countless others. I know it will help you too.

I am here to tell you how to bring clarity into your life, so when you make your goals for your life, they have more significance and connection, and therefore help you create a more meaningful life!

---

1. Mission Statement.com, "Tesla Mission and Vision Statement Analysis," https://mission-statement.com/tesla/#:~:text=Tesla's%20mission%20statement%20is%20%E2%80%9Cto,approaches%20that%20are%20more%20futuristic.

2. Meta Investor Relations, "FAQs," https://investor.fb.com/resources/default.aspx

3. Harvard Business Review, "Not Taking Risks is the Riskiest Career Move of All," https://hbr.org/2015/04/not-taking-risks-is-the-riskiest-career-move-of-all,

CHAPTER 8
BLUEPRINT FOR LIFE: WHEN YOU SEE IT, YOU CAN BE IT

Several years ago as the leader of my daughter's Girl Scout Troop, I reached out to my friend who worked at the Center for Disease Control in Atlanta. He arranged an amazing experience for the girls that they never will forget. The young girls met scientists, learned some of the different types of careers available at the CDC, and even tried on a level 4 hazmat suit. The pièce de resistance was when they met the first ever woman director of the CDC who also said she had been a Girl Scout. The thing I remember most from that spectacular day is what my friend Reggie said to those young girls: "If you can dream it, you can be it."

That phrase is so important because it gave the girls a way to think about what they might be when they grow up. If there aren't women in positions that girls can see as role models they wish to emulate, well, then it might limit what they think is possible. Where have you been limited in your thinking?

Asking the Right Questions

Who do you want to be in life? What do you want to accomplish? What do you really want to achieve on a SOUL level? What will your legacy be?

Those are big questions, and most people do not take the time to reflect on the answers to them. Sometimes they do and then write down a few things but never return to it, let alone measure how they are doing. In other words, they never truly implement plans or a process by which they will achieve what they really want out of life. Many think this is too big of a question.

When I coach people, I always ask, "When you are in the old folks' home in the rocking chair, thinking back on your life, what will you be thinking about?" Now that is a BIG question, so I always help them further along by saying, "It is not the big fancy car you bought or the big, beautiful home that most people reflect upon, but rather the memories they had with their family or the places and experiences that are forever imprinted in their minds that they remember. It is the memories you helped create through experiences, other people, your family and friends, and the way you helped others. So, what will your legacy be?"

This statement always causes people to pause and reflect. And yet, even though I know what a life-changing statement that can be for someone, I never sat down and built out my plan. Here I was, coaching others, and I did not have a plan to share with the people I was coaching to help them achieve their overarching strategic life goals. The next question I would ask was, "How can I help you today?" That brought them right to the place where I could help them with whatever was on their mind at that time. Usually, they have answers within their own minds and just need someone to help pull them out and package it back to them, asking them what their next steps will be to move forward.

Coaching is a wonderful practice. It truly is because it is so incredibly helpful to have someone listen to you as you describe the circumstances you are facing with someone there to validate and repeat back to you what you are saying. There are all kinds of research surrounding that aspect of someone simply giving a person the space to share their feelings, and then that listener validates those feelings. People feel positive after those experiences.

My grandmother was like that without being formally trained. She would sit down with all her grandkids individually as though we were the only people in the world in her life that she cared about. And she listened to us talk. She repeated back what we said, acknowledged our concerns, thoughts, beliefs, and did not give advice but just listened. She genuinely loved us grandkids, and I am incredibly lucky to have had such an amazing example of patience and love in my life.

When I was coaching Brandy, a twenty-year-old who was unsure about which direction to take in terms of college, I challenged her to create her own curriculum. I directed her to research which colleges and universities offered courses she was interested in. Then, I asked her to imagine what type of experiences she wanted to have while in college and to think of the types of courses she would like to take. Armed with this knowledge, I empowered her to go find a college that offered what she was looking for in her life. We often do not take the time to think about what we want. Rather, we go and take what is offered.

When we have more women in all the roles to which we aspire, younger women will see that it is possible because a woman has that role and will plan their journey to achieve the same for themselves. When we do not see women in those roles, we must create the vision for ourselves. If you can dream it, you can be it!

It is important to keep in mind as you think about how to play this game of life that having someone on your team who helps you think about navigating your career and life choices tailored to you is essential. Coaching makes a huge impact on people because it helps us to feel validated and heard, and we as humans crave that experience. But it goes further and asks the question, "What will you do about that?" Many of us are seeking advice from someone else. I have been there and have done that. "Just tell me what to do!" has been spoken in prayer many a time by me alone. Good coaches do not tell you the answer; they help you figure it out.

If you had figured out who you want to be in this life, what you wanted to accomplish on a soul level, and knew what legacy you wanted to leave behind, you might still have scenarios where it helps to have someone else work through a problem with you (where you do all the work, of course, and they ask the right questions to help you get there). This book might help you better understand how you want to show up and get clear on the impact of your actions because you are working on those things every day. However, there are many reasons to meet with a coach or therapist to work through certain areas where you might get stuck and to learn better ways to handle similar situations in the future. This book and the corresponding planner are in no way intended to be a substitute for seeking medical advice and/or mental health.

Coaches are great because, even as you progress in your journey, you might find that the things you will need a coach for are to learn how someone has done something similar in the past and can successfully guide you on the things that you are trying to do. The net result is that you get coaching to help you get started or learn from them so you can accomplish your goal more quickly.

There are folks who might need something more than what a coach is able to help with, so they might seek out a therapist to work through those types of matters.

Implementing the ideas from this book does not mean that you will never need coaches or therapists. They are integral to our overall wellness. The purpose of this book is to help you learn how to focus on those high-level questions of who you want to be. What will your legacy be? Because guess what? You get to create it. Along the way of working out the answers to all of these questions, you might come to the realization that you are stuck in an area and have not been able to move past it. Therapists or coaches might be the right avenue to pursue in those cases. Or, you might decide that you want to work with a therapist as you go through the steps outlined in this book and the associated planner. It is designed for you and what you need to find your truth. In Chapter 20, there is more information about getting in the game with a coach. For now, the new rules for the game could include getting a coach to help you to see possibilities you might not have considered before.

Make Goals

Usually, people suggest creating goals, then achieving them. There is a lot of research indicating that people who write down their goals have a much higher chance of achieving them. That is amazing! But usually, our goals are tactical in that they help us save for practical things like retirement, a new house, or vacation. And those are great goals to have! But ask someone to write out goals to achieve their legacy and they might blankly stare back at you.

How can you plan for something you have not defined? This scenario is a big disconnect most people have in their lives. They keep hitting goals and making plans, doing the daily grind, but they still feel empty inside and unfulfilled.

Let us say you make a goal to save money and that you want to make a certain amount of money in your career by the age of 30. So, you plan and save and finally reach your goal at the age of 29. One year ahead of schedule. Congratulations! Cool, now what?

Was that fulfilling? Did you celebrate? Is that a legacy goal? It might be, but what is next after that? Do you keep setting higher and higher monetary goals to achieve over and over again? You most likely will find it to be an empty promise over the long run. Many people do. There are many rich unhappy people in this world.

If you are lucky enough to do some soul-searching after that initial monetary success, you might figure out that your next goal is not related to money at all. It might be because when you made that monetary goal happen, you realized there must be more to life than money. That is when you might be closer to your truth. The reality is that most of us do not do that.

Most of us chase after life rather than being in the driver's seat of our own lives. Being in the driver's seat means being in charge, knowing where we want to go and the reason why we want to go there. Being in charge of our lives, driving the car of life, to the destination of our choice is important. There were too many times when I allowed others to sit in the driver's seat for me and direct my life. That was never a good feeling, and why on earth would I hand over my power like that to someone else? I learned that I was extremely unhappy in that scenario and vowed never to live that way again. It leads to unhappiness. How many of us do that? It is part of what we are taught. We must overcome that tendency and think about the importance of our own lives and where we want to drive our cars. Taking the time to focus on your life through the system explained in this book will help you gain clarity on those areas of your life that you are unclear about or maybe have never explored before.

Taking the time to do soul-searching and reflection will help you gain clarity—so whatever goals you decide are important are yours and yours alone. This will truly help you reach your life's purpose.

In Chapter 15 - Getting Clear, you will be guided through the steps needed to achieve clarity.

Once you get super clear and begin applying the system by creating plans that support your goals, you will start to see positive changes in your life that you did not realize were part of your initial goal. For example, in my case, I made it a goal to write this book to achieve my mission of helping people live their best lives. As I started tracking my daily goals toward writing the book, I discovered that I needed to make myself healthier. How could I offer advice to others when I was not in the best shape I could be? Therefore, I began walking 10,000 steps every day. I also began eating much healthier. It was not my initial plan or goal at the time to do either, but when I made that realization, I added those tasks to my daily plan. As I followed the practice, new goals started to surface. The side benefits can be amazing! But don't be surprised when your goals start to expand.

After you have been conducting this practice for some time, you will notice that your goals keep changing. You might start by stating, "I want to help people by cooking healthy food and sharing." Then, as you keep moving forward to that goal, you realize, *Wait a minute, not only do I want to do that, but now I want to start a charitable organization that brings healthy foods to under-funded schools.*

The main thing to note is that this is a practice and not a one-and-done scenario where you figure out this secret thing and that is the end of the journey. Once you reach or come close to a goal, you change. Your worldview might change. You feel great that you accomplished this amazing goal! But the next day, you might start losing your mojo again. Either you did not celebrate reaching that goal or you need to set a new one. As Miley Cyrus sings about in her song "The Climb," there is always going to be another mountain to reach. It is not about the mountains; it is about the climb. Therefore, you will need to go back and conduct the exercises again to maintain your clarity around your purpose. It truly is a journey.

Make a Plan!

"A goal without a plan is just a wish." –Antoine de Saint-Exupéry

Some begin this journey for truth without guideposts to help them figure out what they are seeking. Why are guideposts important? They help you stay on course. I think of it like the pillars in boating whether in a lake, or in my case, the ocean. They keep you in the lines and on the right path so you don't hit a reef. Guideposts guide your efforts. They are much broader than goals.

The guideposts I found most helpful are from the Vedas. The Vedas are the "most ancient Hindu scriptures, written in early Sanskrit and containing hymns, philosophy…" according to Dictionary.com. I find these guideposts to be the most meaningful to me and hope they help you as well.

Well-meaning friends and family will suggest you follow this path forward in your life: plan your college career, plan your business career, plan your family, plan your trips, plan for college (for your kids), plan for retirement. Then, you are done with life and waiting around…for what? A lot of planning, but to what end? Sure, these are important items to make sure you plan for, and they certainly are necessary. Equally as necessary is a plan for your soul's purpose. Creating a purpose and using your guideposts will help you navigate a plan for who you want to be in this world. A plan for leaving a legacy behind is probably the most important plan in your life. Very few people in this world figure this part out. You are in the minority, so congratulate yourselves for showing up, reading this book, and figuring out how to make your blueprint for life a reality.

There is more emphasis these days on human-centered design. In the past in software development, many new programs were created by developers who thought they were delivering great solutions, but it turns out that they forgot to put the user of the system in the driver's seat. The developers forgot to ask if the software worked in a way that best served the people who would be using the tool daily. As a result, the outcome many times was that the end-users simply had to use the tool that the software engineers built because the company had already spent millions of dollars on it. The end-users would have to create workarounds or take more time to accomplish certain tasks than before. It was a mess in some cases! In other words, we planned for the wrong things. Not with bad intentions, but rather, we forgot who we were building it for. If there was a strategy in place that the developers referred to as their guideposts while building the solution, the outcome might have been different.

Our savings and tactical plans can be the same. We plan for and work hard for that raise, but we realize once we get there that it is still unfulfilling.

Now, we have a human-centered design that keeps the end-user at the heart of everything we build. We want the tool to create efficiencies, not make it more difficult for the users to do their jobs. The result is happier end-users, but we still need all of the guideposts to help us stay on track.

Without a life purpose to guide you, your goals and action plans may not be fulfilling.

There are pillars in life that help act as guideposts because you need all of them to live a full life. These pillars and their importance are shared in more detail in Chapter 13. The pillars are intertwined, meaning each goal you set will likely tick all four pillars or at least set you on the path toward developing a more meaningful life.

The mistake most people make is to go start planning their career/lives as a first step. The problem is that you are then planning without knowing who you are first. What is the end result? Unhappiness. Why? Because you are planning someone else's idea of a career/life. Society, family, friends all will tell you what your life should be, either by example or by clearly stating it. But even they get it wrong unless they have done what I am suggesting you do first, which is: Ask the right questions, get clear on who you want to be in life, and determine your guideposts (those things that guide your life journey). Then you will be able to plan YOUR life. Not some construct of what society says your life should be.

CHAPTER 9
OPPORTUNITIES, NOT TASKS

During my corporate career, I was part of a trio of women working on an important session at a Fortune 100 company to teach women about the current environment in which they found themselves, and then to share what leaders could do about it. One of the women researched and shared this notion of women getting opportunities and not tasks. This was a new concept for me. I have been a women's rights advocate for decades at this point. I wanted to make the workplace better for my daughters so that when they entered the workforce, they would find themselves on a more equal playing ground at work. Well, I am still advocating, teaching, mentoring, coaching and now writing this book to help women move ahead. Some things were great experiences for me, like this session we were leading, but many of them were tasks that men did not take on and only women were asked or volunteered to lead the work. Once I started thinking about this concept, I realized how many things I had signed up to lead that got me thanks but no reward. I agree that not everything should be done just so you can get ahead, but think about this:

More women volunteer for tasks than men, and more men get opportunities as opposed to women.

Once I realized this, I was very angry. I was upset with myself for not having made this realization. But I faced it head-on and started saying "no" to those tasks that were not moving me forward in my career. I had spent so much not realizing that if I wanted opportunities, I had to be strategic in how I went about asking for them. If things were equally split across men and women (tasks, opportunities, pay, management roles, etc.), then yes, I would take on my fair share. But look around. That is not the current environment in most Fortune 500 companies. I would argue that it is not the norm in most companies. Here's what the research says.

Harvard Business Review did a study and found women more likely to volunteer for tasks versus men. "Our research suggests that this reluctant volunteer is more likely to be female than male. Across field and laboratory studies, we found that women volunteer for these 'non-promotable' tasks more than men; that women are more frequently asked to take such tasks on; and that when asked, they are more likely to say yes."

My boss' manager had listed out activities that he needed his team to work on as they kicked off the new year. This list was shared with my leaders. The activities that had the least value were taken on by my manager. The activities that had direct revenue impact were given to all the male leaders. These activities, when delivered successfully, would be included in the performance evaluation and resulting performance bonuses for these male leaders. The activities my boss received were very time-consuming, with no direct link to improvements—monetarily or otherwise. This was my first clear indication that this phenomenon was happening in my world, and I was going to do something about it for myself.

Before you go change the world (which I hope you do!), you

must become aware of what is actually happening in the world in which we live. There is institutionalized bias against women and diverse populations. In fact, women of color succeed at far fewer rates than white women. In order to succeed, you need to know what game you are playing. It doesn't help to be out on the field, ready to play baseball when the rest of the team is playing football.

Women are 50% of the population and usually 50% of the workforce in any given company, and yet only 20% of top leadership positions are filled by women, as the McKinsey study clearly points out. I encourage you to review the articles co-authored by McKinsey and Lean-in.org for more data. But why is this happening?

One of the main components is this phenomenon of women getting tasks and men getting opportunities. Here's what *Harvard Business Review* determined from their research:

"These results instead suggest that the real driver [referring to the disparity between men and women on taking on tasks] was a shared understanding or expectation that women would volunteer more than men. In a mixed-sex group, men will hold back on volunteering while women, in turn, will volunteer to ensure that the task is done. But in single-sex groups, this changes—men and women volunteer equally. In these groups, men know they have to step forward if they want to find a volunteer, and women expect other women to volunteer, making them less compelled to do so themselves. Interestingly, in women's groups, the volunteering ends up being shared equally across 10 rounds, while in men's groups it tends to fall on the same men each time."

Further, they studied how managers delegate tasks and found that "women received 44% more requests to volunteer than men in mixed-sex groups. Intriguingly, the gender of the manager did not make a difference: Both male and female managers were more likely to ask a woman to volunteer than a man. This was apparently a wise decision: women were also more likely to say yes. A request to volunteer was accepted by men 51% of the time and by women 76% of the time."[1]

What are the consequences of taking on tasks? There can be major career impacts on women if they do take on tasks that keep them busy and their calendars filled. If their focus was on tasks rather than work, that was more likely to lead to promotions, bonuses, or both. As a result, it will take longer for women to get ahead.

Women have the same level of education as men and yet we do not see an equitable balance in leadership. When there are institutionalized biases against women who get saddled with tasks that take them away from opportunities that directly lead to promotions, of course, women will progress more slowly than men. Other studies that show these "systemic gender differences in how work is allocated" are not just from the *Harvard Business Review* but also from people like Irene De Pater and colleagues, Sara Mitchell, and Vicki Hesli, and many others that back up these facts.

How does this show up in everyday life? If you are in a meeting and are asked to get the coffee, schedule all the meetings, take meeting notes, etc., politely decline and volunteer a co-worker. I have an entire chapter devoted to saying "no" that goes into much more detail. But in this scenario, you could mention that you have done this already and would like to give someone else a chance to take notes, get coffee, or schedule the next meeting. Call someone out by name and look at the person who is asking you to do that task, not the person you are volunteering with.

Bottom line—we need to be the change we want to see. But the first step is awareness. The second step is action.

So, now we know one of the reasons that we do not move ahead—tasks versus opportunities. What can we do about it?

We need to overcome societal norms. How? By becoming the change we want to see. By transforming ourselves first. First, become aware. Look around; are you volunteering for activities that do not lead to a promotion? Look at the work you are doing right now. What has been assigned as a top priority by your manager? Is it a task, or will it lead to measurable results? If it is a task, think about delegating it or finishing it up quickly, and then make plans to acquire a project that has more opportunity—one that drives impact to the bottom line.

When women start seeing the opportunities that will create true growth, then leaders will start valuing their contribution, and women will start getting more promotions.

Think about how you can move your career to the next level, and keep yourself focused on carefully selecting those things that will bring you there. This is not to say that you are always going to be in a position to turn down tasks, but be mindful of how the tasks are assigned, and point out to your manager the fact that the requests could be split more equitably across the team in a way that shows you are team player. More about that in the chapter related to saying "no."

It is not your role to teach the world how to behave, but you can teach others how you wish to be treated, and that includes standing up for yourself in a no-nonsense manner when it comes to being assigned tasks in your career. There are ways to look at it as a favor where you negotiate with your boss, if you do take on this task, that he or she will give you a coveted project, for example. There are ways to negotiate and ask for what you want. Going heads-down and doing a good job is not a strategy to help you move forward in your career.

---

1. Harvard Business Review, "Why Woman Volunteer for Tasks That Don't Lead to Promotions," https://hbr.org/2018/07/why-women-volunteer-for-tasks-that-dont-lead-to-promotions

CHAPTER 10
SETTING BOUNDARIES

Setting boundaries is essential to ensure that people treat us the way we expect to be treated. It is not always as obvious as putting up a fence around ourselves and making decisions about who can come in and who can't, but it is making certain we think about the behaviors we will and will not accept. What happens when someone mistreats you? What will you do, and how will you react to let the other person know that their behavior is unacceptable? Some of us are better than others at this concept of boundaries.

Julia Horvath penned a great article, "How To Set Healthy Boundaries — A Compassionate Guide for Women," about the types of boundaries and how to set them.[1] In this article, the author states with respect to traditional gender roles, "Implicit social rules and gender roles make boundaries by definition more difficult to set for women than for men." The author continues explaining that women are taught that any show of aggression is deemed unfeminine. This teaching makes it difficult for many women to set boundaries that protect themselves because they fear appearing too forceful and unladylike.

We must address how to set boundaries for ourselves and ask for what we want. As children, when a parent says "no" to a request for candy, for example, we might have cried and asked repeatedly for that candy yet still not received it. As adults, we learn that we cannot behave that way, and when someone says "no," we respect that decision. We might question why the person came to that conclusion, but when someone says "no," we accept the decision. If we do not accept someone saying "no" to us, we might have an unhealthy boundary.

So how does having a lack of boundaries show up? It might be that we do not speak up for ourselves at work. We allow others to dominate a conversation and are hesitant to interject our ideas that could contribute positively to the organization. The net result of that timid behavior is that you might be overlooked for promotions or continue to take on tasks because you are fearful of saying "no" to anyone who asks.

The unladylike construct is a double bind because when we do speak up for ourselves and interject our suggestions with ideas in meetings and conversations, there are times when we are viewed as being too forceful. Men might view a woman speaking up in a meeting as unfeminine and then place her into that category in the eyes of her boss and peers. Because the gender norms are still ingrained in many men and women, the only path forward is to learn to be yourself, state the facts without emotion, set boundaries on how you wish to be treated, and call people out when they cross over them. Easier said than done, right?

I will be honest, changing my mindset about boundaries was very difficult because I was just embarking on my career in an era when women had minimal rights or respect in the workplace. It was also around this time when the movie *Nine to Five* came out. For those who have not seen this movie, the premise is that three working women find themselves in unhealthy, sexist office environments where they ultimately manage to turn things around in a humorous way. The situations these women found themselves in within the workforce were real for many women who, at the time, were fighting for equal rights. The goal of the movie was to bring to light the unequal treatment that was taking place in the workforce. It was based on a real organization founded in 1973, Nine to Five, which is now "…one of the largest, most respected national membership organizations of working women in the U.S., dedicated to putting working women's issues on the public agenda."

The same societal gender norms are taught today; however, people are more careful about how they exhibit these beliefs. Women are still paid less than men. Therefore, for things to change, we must change. But how?

My recommendation is to start at home. If you live with a partner, it is important to establish equal workloads when it comes to watching the children, cleaning the house, and running errands. By starting at home, the newly acquired boundaries will begin to show up at work over time. It is not about getting this perfect or right. Sometimes, we swing to one side of the spectrum and then the other until we land in the middle with how we stand up for ourselves. Most of us just want the job done when it comes to household chores. Therefore, we just do the work. However, ensuring our home lives are equitable in household chores is important. The same thing applies in the work environment.

How can we apply boundaries to ensure we do not accept tasks without getting any opportunities? How can you ensure your balance at home is made more equitable before you expect change at work? The only person who is responsible for making change is you. Once you start stating what you want and enforcing boundaries structured internally by you and for you, then you will see changes occurring. The problem is that the solution is simple, but the actions for most are difficult. Shifting our mindsets to realize we have worth will help us to realize that all household chores need to be equitably split.

There will be things you enjoy more than your partner and vice versa, but offer to take the car in for an oil change, mow the lawn, etc. Look at the actual work and break it down in terms of the daily amount of time it takes, weekly amount of time, monthly, annually. Start with daily chores. Write them out, step by step: packing lunch for kids, dishes, grocery shopping, cooking, baths, homework, sweeping, vacuuming, emptying dishwasher, cleaning bathroom, making beds, laundry, etc. Then, divide the chores equitably with your partner. You might start with a list, approach your partner, share the list, and ask your partner to help you divide the chores equitably. In her book *FAIR PLAY*, Eve Rodsky gives clear examples of how this might be accomplished. She states that when she first made her list, her husband didn't suddenly change his behavior. She made a game of it that she used to make the needed changes in gender norm perceptions. I highly encourage people to read this book because the methodology helps to showcase the reasons why women are still doing most household chores today. And it provides great examples of steps to take to turn that around in real life. As Eve Rodsky states, "All time is created equal."

To summarize, setting boundaries is imperative to successfully navigating life. You reduce feelings of resentment, and your needs get met. For some, this is easy. For many, it is difficult. Reach out to me for coaching if this is an area in which you find yourself struggling.

---

1. Julia Horvath, "How To Set Healthy Boundaries—A Compassionate Guide for Women," https://betterhumans.pub/how-to-set-healthy-boundaries-a-compassionate-guide-for-women-98a509d853a8

SECTION IV: THE NEW GAME

GET IN THE GAME

CHAPTER 11
SOUL SAVINGS: ARE YOU WILLING TO INVEST?

"All around me are familiar faces
Worn out places, worn out faces.
Bright and early for the daily races,
Going nowhere, going nowhere."
–Orzabal Roland, "Mad World"

It is a mad world, especially if you do not reflect on your experiences, life's purpose, goals, and dreams. It is difficult to fit into a world where most people are stuck in their own boxes, not taking the time to invest in themselves. When we do not know who we are, we likely make random choices, and allow life to pull us along in the current. In that scenario, a person can be swept in the current of someone else's goals and dreams and not our own. What if we were to take a step outside of the water, stand on the shoreline of the river of life, and observe the water going by? One of the best ways to uncover your soul's purpose is to write a journal.

Why a Written Journal?

That is a great question! There is a lot of research that indicates that the act of manually writing is the most effective means of helping to reduce anxiety while helping to strengthen our mind-body connection.

According to this article published on PsychCentral.com, several studies discuss how writing is "associated with fewer symptoms of anxiety and depression" and outline the many benefits journaling creates. https://psychcentral.com/stress/how-to-begin-journaling-for-stress-relief[1]

In her article, "Expressive Writing for Physical and Mental Health," author Sharon K. Farber, PhD., shares, "Psychologist James Pennebaker (1991) has written about this in *Opening Up: The Healing Power of Confiding in Others*, in which he describes the numerous scientific studies he has done on the benefits of expressive writing, either through speaking or writing."[2]

Writing about and expressing your emotions on paper is cathartic and easier for most people than speaking about them. However, it is important to remember that writing will not magically help you overcome trauma, divorce, and other similar occurrences. It is designed for use when you are working through anxiety or if you have so much on your mind that you cannot focus; taking those thoughts from mind to paper relieves tension for a lot of people.

If you do not love writing, the suggestion is to try it out, and the more you do it, the easier it gets. Take the time to notice how you feel afterward and write about it. With the vast amount of evidenced-based research to back up this point, it is in my hopes you get into the habit of using a journal to help you experience these same positive outcomes.

Why Are We Not Willing to Work On Ourselves?

I often picked up a journal and put it down again without thinking about it. Why was it so difficult to write down how my day had gone, what exciting new thing happened, or anything else? In her article, "How Journaling Heals: There's No 'Write' Way to Journal," January 11, 2016, by Laurie Leinwand, MA, LPC, on the GoodTherapy.org website, she explains reasons why folks are hesitant to write. It can be that they fear someone will read their innermost thoughts and judge them, or it could be the fear they have of not trusting that their own thoughts are "right." I have started and stopped journaling numerous times. I wrote on individual pieces of paper, then tore them up and threw them away. Why did I not want to reflect on my life? Maybe because it was a reflection of me, and I did not want to see my life's reflection. Was I afraid of what I would learn or ashamed of how I had acted? Or was I disappointed in where I was? Ultimately, those thoughts may have crossed into the deep recesses of my subconscious, but they never rose to the surface. I stayed on a superficial level and never took the time to think about it more deeply.

As I began using my practice of journaling in earnest, daily, sticking with it no matter what, I learned the truth: I never developed my north star. That is why I needed to go back to the beginning and journal about what I ultimately wanted in my life. If I had thought about what I wanted, then that thought was only in passing. I never applied any framework or goals to how I would achieve it. If I am honest with myself, I never wrote anything down, never explored myself that deeply, and then I wondered why my life was so unfulfilling. The practice of journaling about my hopes and dreams and what I wanted out of life helped shape my mission statement more fully. I developed my north star! The practice of journaling and asking the questions shared in Chapter 7 is what will help you not only to stay on track, but to stay true to your north star.

Journaling can help you uncover why you may not feel like you have a full life. So, let's uncover why your life might feel unfulfilled. Most people do the daily grind, whatever that is in their alleged time of life. Go to school, get a job, get married, have kids, retire, and boom—you are done with your life. Sure, there are good memories along the way, but many people know there is more to life than that. Or they believe that it is just our lot of life and do not seek something better. We are meant to go to the daily grind and then we retire. That is all we get. That does not have to be your fate.

All the research indicates that if you put in the work of focusing on yourself and getting clear on your purpose, you will get results that lead to having a more fulfilled life. According to the University of Rochester, "Keeping a journal helps you create order when your world feels like it's in chaos. You get to know yourself by revealing your most private fears, thoughts, and feelings... Look forward to your journaling time. And know that you're doing something good for your mind and body."

Contemplating a problem and experiencing stress? Studies find writing in a journal can assist in determining the source of your stress or anxiety. You can implement a plan to address these problems and minimize your stress through your journal. [3]

In one study conducted in 2006, nearly 100 young adults were tasked with spending 15 minutes journaling or drawing about an event they found stressful, or writing about their daily plans, twice during one week. Those in the study who journaled experienced the biggest reduction in symptoms like depression, anxiety, and hostility. This reduction in symptoms was especially significant if they were very distressed from the start of the study. This finding occurred even though 80 percent had rarely journaled about their feelings and only 61 percent felt comfortable doing so. [4]

Then the question becomes, "Why do we avoid journaling?"

Over time when we journal, we can review what we were thinking and assess the reasons for the thoughts we had at the time. Reasoning out our thoughts and considering how we might do things differently to get a better result takes work and dedication. It also makes us sit in our (maybe) not-so-great behavior and look at the root cause. No one is saying this is easy, but it works. It helps us to grow and change. Also, "…in the long term, we can expect to cultivate a greater sense of meaning as well as better health. Various studies have found that people who do a bout of journaling have fewer doctor visits in the following half-year, and reduced symptoms of chronic disease like asthma and arthritis."[5]

Writing can be a huge boost to our mental health, even if we are not working through a traumatic experience. "It can make us more aware (and self-aware!) and help us detect sneaky, unhealthy patterns in our thoughts and behaviors. It allows us to take more control over our lives and puts things in perspective. Further, it can help us shift from a negative mindset to a more positive one, especially about ourselves (Robinson, 2017)."[6]

So, where does that leave us in this mad world? We get to choose our path to a large degree. The fact is, for me, I cannot leave corporate America right now because I do need to keep a roof over my head and my kids' heads. I do need to save for retirement. But in searching for my life's purpose, I found a lot of very creative and rewarding things along the way. For one, writing. I never pictured myself as a writer, but here I am writing a self-help book based on my personal experience. It is at once rewarding and fulfilling. I believe from the bottom of my heart that it will help so many people find meaning in their lives and live more fully. As the old saying goes, "If I help only one person through this book, then I have done my job." I believe that statement, and I needed to get this book published and out there to help others on their journey.

The bottom line is that journaling works. So why not try it? What if you do it every day, answering targeted questions to help you get clear on what your life goals are? I can say that I have moved further along in my soul-searching journey because of implementing the practices shared with you in this book.

The world may be mad, but we can bring some clarity and fulfillment into our lives through this work. I am living proof.

It is time to invest in yourself and in your soul. No matter what happened earlier in life or even yesterday, right now, you have the opportunity to move your self-awareness and your life toward more positive outcomes. The question now is, "Are you ready to invest in your soul?"

I hope the answer is "yes." I believe in this so strongly and want you to take the step forward, too. I have worked with countless clients who have implemented these practices and have achieved great success, peace of mind, and led more fulfilling lives as a result. This practice is working for so many, and I know it will work for you.

I am grateful you are on this journey and look forward to your results when you begin investing in your soul.

---

1. Farber, Dr. Sharon K., PsychCentral.com, "How to Begin Journaling for Stress Relief." https://psychcentral.com/stress/how-to-begin-journaling-for-stress-relief

2. Psychology Today, "Expressive Writing for Physical and Mental Health," https://www.psychologytoday.com/us/blog/the-mind-body-connection/201603/expressive-writing-physical-and-mental-health

3. University of Rochester Medical Center Health Encyclopedia, "Journaling for Mental Health," https://www.urmc.rochester.edu/encyclopedia/content.aspx?ContentID=4552&ContentTypeID=1

4. Greater Good Magazine, "How Journaling Can Help You in Hard Times," https://greatergood.berkeley.edu/article/item/how_journaling_can_help_you_in_hard_times

5. Greater Good Magazine, "How Journaling Can Help You in Hard Times," https://greatergood.berkeley.edu/article/item/how_journaling_can_help_you_in_hard_times

6. Positive Psychology, "83 Benefits of Journaling for Depression, Anxiety, and Stress," https://positivepsychology.com/benefits-of-journaling/

CHAPTER 12

DISCIPLINE: THE WORLD'S GREATEST DRUG

Discipline is an amazing and unlikely topic when thinking about it from the perspective of a drug. Those who use illegal drugs are not typically associated with discipline. However, users of illegal drugs and alcoholics often hide their habits from others and partake in secret. That takes a lot of discipline to get the drugs or alcohol, bring them into the house, hide it from family members, and still manage to use the drug or drink the alcoholic beverage without being discovered. It takes a lot of thought and planning, not to mention management.

We typically do not think about those aspects of habits. Habits are just habits; we all have them. I like to have my morning coffee before the rest of the family gets out of bed. I enjoy the quiet time where I can reflect in my journal in solitude. I have dog duty at that time of day, and I love seeing my big buddy every morning as I come downstairs, where he greets me like he hasn't seen me in years. I savor those moments and that time. But it takes a certain amount of planning and discipline to get up at the same time, make a pot of joe, feed the dog, and get everything settled so I can have that time for gathering my thoughts and thinking about the day ahead. If I do not get up early enough, I will not have enough time for myself, so I get up early so I can conduct the actions around my coffee/writing habit. Most would agree that this ritual is a good habit other than the coffee part. I would, too. Plus, I am not giving up coffee.

Please remember that this is a journey and a daily practice. It works if you keep doing it. This routine is an example of an issue I came up against, and I wanted to devote a chapter to discussing how we create our own roadblocks to success. One of the best ways to get through that is to realize we need discipline to make ourselves focus on this important work. It is one of the most important elements in the program and in life! We need to develop self-discipline to get things done.

I recently listened to a podcast show called *Hardcore Humanism* with Dr. Mike. It is a great podcast for those of you interested in exploring humanistic psychology as Dr. Mike invites a wide range of interesting people as his guests and interviews them to learn how they "break convention" and lead their own lives outside of what we consider to be normal.

On one of his episodes, he was interviewing singer and song-writer Mod Sun. Mod said that, for the first time in his life, he was learning discipline because he stopped his addiction to cocaine and now is addicted to running. If you think about it, there are ritualistic principles to an addiction. You must think about how you will manage your high and give a lot of thought to even getting the drug. Dr. Mike stated, "Drugs have no major label marketing and yet we find them."

There is a discipline involved to even getting the drugs to get their needs met. That same discipline can help you do positive things in your life, like taking up running, which is what Mod Sun started doing. Mod went on to say, "Addiction to the positive things are the best addictions you could ever have!"

It is important to incorporate the discipline of this daily prac-tice of writing in your planning journal. When you find yourself not conducting daily reflection, you should ask yourself, "Why is that?"

It takes work and effort to maintain our habits. What if we could turn one habit that is not serving us into another one that does? It is the same amount of work, right? Many people share how they stopped smoking and suddenly gained weight because the habit of having something in their mouths was satisfying. If it could no longer be a cigarette, they would go to the refrigerator and find something to satisfy that need. They replace one habit for another. For example, sitting down to write in a journal every day will take discipline. It must be a habit that becomes part of your daily process. Research shows how the act of physically getting ideas out of your head and onto paper can give many people a better night's sleep. Once their thoughts are written down on paper, journaling releases their minds to relax and go to sleep. Therefore, making journaling a habit will keep you on track and you might get better sleep as a result!

The issue most people have is that they succumb to having that cigarette, drink, food, etc., instead of using discipline to write in their journal first. After you have gotten your feelings out on paper, ask yourself if you really do need that cigarette, drink, food, etc. Journaling about your triggers can help you learn to break the cycle of addiction to these things that do not serve us. This behavior truly takes discipline to achieve. It's a small step to take the time to write first, but the results are incredible.

Your mind is extremely powerful, and sometimes, the act of writing helps to relieve your mind of a few things it is trying to hold onto. When you write down all of your thoughts onto paper, it helps to free up your mind, enabling it to relax. The result is that your mind feels calmer because all the energy and effort it took to think about and make sense of the multitude of thoughts swirling in your head has now been documented on paper. You can read it back and make sense of it. Your mind no longer has to keep track of the thoughts that are piling up.

Our thoughts at times can also start spinning around, almost like a hamster wheel of sorts, where all the effort to keep the wheel moving doesn't result in reaching any destination. We can work ourselves up into a frenzy of thought and worry and it keeps looping around so you feel like you cannot turn it off. This is behavior is anxiety. It is a terrible feeling and quite scary at times. But when you practice getting out your journal and writing your thoughts down as they occur at the end of each day, or when your thoughts become worrisome, it takes the swirl of thoughts and energy out of your mind and into a document that you can review. Once it is on paper, you can reflect and think about all that you have written down. For some, it is similar to sharing your concerns with a therapist; once you share, you immediately start feeling better. There is truth to the phrase, "I feel better now that I have that off of my chest." For the most part, people feel better once they share a concern with someone else. Journaling can help you get your concerns, thoughts, feelings, and more documented on paper. The result is you are clearer, you sleep better, and you can now relax and think through the problem or situation that might have been tangled up in your mind.

Here is the proposal: Are you ready to invest in yourself? And if you answered "yes" to that question, are you now willing to do the work to make journaling a daily habit?

Growth is uncomfortable but moving through it is exciting when you see what happens on the other end of it. You can come out stronger and more confident. Maybe not immediately but years later when you reflect on how the event changed you.

This is powerful. When you journal, you are capturing these moments in your life. By having it down on paper, you can review it, add to it, edit it, whatever is needed to ensure you look at your life. Your life belongs to you. You are the caretaker of it. Please do not turn over this responsibility to someone else, some societal norm, or some dominating ex-husband (wait, did I write that out loud?!?). Your life is yours to live, and you get to decide if you will put in the discipline to take steps toward habits that serve you positively.

The best advice I was given when trying to make a healthy habit change was to make sure I planned. Know you will want to go off track and not take the time to journal. But try to have the journal beside your bed with the pen ready to write. Try leaving your journal open on the page for the day the night before. In other words, make it super easy to pick it up and write in it. I have heard similar tactics for making running easy, such as putting your running shoes and clothes close to your bed so that you see them upon waking. These little tricks do make a difference to help your mind not find excuses for you to carry through with your habit—that habit that you said you were going to take on and do every day. You do it every day because it is investing in your soul. That is the habit that I am referring to you. If you keep this mind-set, you will go far.

Asking for support also makes a huge difference. Asking someone to give you feedback or to listen to you as you work through a problem or even reaching out to a therapist or coach for help on any issue that might arise during this practice is vitally important. We are social creatures and are meant to be with others who support us. Do not be shy about asking for help.

Take time out for healthy activities that move your body. I will cover more on this topic later in the book but think about ways in which playing a game of hide-n-go-seek with the kids is not only fun but full of calorie-burning activities! Or you can walk your dog or go for a walk in the neighborhood. I actually have to drive to another area to walk because there are no sidewalks in my immediate community. Therefore, it is a big commitment. I remind myself that I am investing in myself, and I am worth that time and energy.

Tracking your progress is very important. Find a daily tracker where you can write in how well you think you did at the end of the day. Be honest with yourself. This exercise is intended to help you see where you are in your process. You will figure out ways to improve. The trend should be upward over the long term, but do not worry about the ups and downs of each day. That is normal for everybody. We do not achieve perfection. We aspire to be on the journey to try.

Another great tactic that is shown to work by all the great self-help gurus and in many popular books is to imagine the future. Put yourself into the shoes of yourself in the future and begin to imagine what it feels like to reach that goal. For this book, I imagined someone (a woman like me—before I began this journey) who was searching for meaning and thinking to herself, *Is this all there is?* I imagined she was reading the words in my future book and thinking about what she was feeling and how the concepts in the book were helping her to move forward in her life just as this practice has helped me. Then, I imagine her writing to me on my website or a comment on the book ratings where she writes about how much this process has helped her.

It is my hope that this book helps more than one person, but again, even if it is one person that I help, this effort would be completely worth it! It is worth it already, as the act of simply writing it is bringing even more insight and clarity to my personal journey.

Remember to create space and time to reward yourself for all that you are doing in your life. Many days when I think about gratitude, I thank myself for following through with this practice of being thankful. I am grateful to be on the journey, and I am thankful every day for it. In addition, it is helpful to reward yourself with a new pen or even a party for completing a goal that you set in your planner. I know someone whose boss celebrated with her for getting a certification that she had been striving to achieve and tracking the results in her planner. It is important to celebrate and recognize the good work, the time, and devotion you placed into achieving that goal. Reward yourself. It will help you to bring closure as well as give you a moment to savor and return to when you are struggling with a future goal. It helps build and solidify your credibility yourself. You might say to yourself when the going gets tough, "I did this! I have done this. I will do this again!" Building confidence in yourself and proving that you can achieve goals (even little wins are important; they still move you forward!) is a recognized way to help you stay on track toward achieving your goals.

The last piece of advice is to be patient. Results do not always show up overnight. Instant gratification is a problem in our society today with our smart phones, apps, and ability to find the answer to many questions so quickly. The act of journaling and sticking with this system is a practice. Just like the practice of learning to read or run, you must practice it to get better. Confidence-building is a practice. Please remember to practice every day and make it your drug of choice.

If your habit is journaling, you will certainly reap the benefits of that habit.

Habits

Organize your habits, write about them, and add them to your daily planner. When you write the steps that you will take onto paper, it makes it a more tangible goal. But not just any steps will do. Here are some ways in which you can create an effective habit for yourself:

1. Connect your habit to a habit that already exists. If you already have one habit, try tying the new one to the one that already exists. Let's say my new habit is that I want to do is meditation, and a bad habit I want to stop doing is eating late at night. I also want to get a good night's sleep. So, let's break down what this might look like.

2. Instead of going to the kitchen to make a late-night snack (existing habit), I will_____ (insert your reward of choice here).
3. I will _____ (An example might be: I will listen to a guided meditation on YouTube for 10 minutes while I lay in bed before I go to sleep).
4. Now, create a reward for doing it.
5. After I wake up the next morning (because I got an amazing night of sleep because the guided meditation was effective in winding me down from the day), I will _____
6. Make up a reward. It could be that you give yourself a few minutes extra time on the alarm clock or allow yourself to relax and listen to music for a few minutes before getting out of bed to start the day.

This technique helps you think about how you can form new habits from existing ones. I chose a bad habit I wanted to replace with a good one. But you might tie a good habit with another good habit. Let's say you want to get in more exercise during the day. You might do the following:

1. Every day when I walk outside to get the mail, I will take a run around the block before picking up the mail.
2. I will <Insert reward here>. It could be that you make a cup of tea and sit on the couch for 10 minutes listening to music while opening the mail. For me, I usually grab the mail and stand while I open it as quickly as I can and disburse accordingly (trash/pay/needs action). But maybe it is a reward to make a new ritual to slow down with a cup of tea and not rush through the process.

I think those ideas will help you think of ways to add new habits or replace ones that no longer serve you.

If we take the time to plan out how we can incorporate little changes into our regular routines, we can make a big impact. It is when we don't plan that things go sideways or rarely get done. This idea was inspired by the book *Atomic Habits: An Easy & Proven Way to Build Good Habits & Break Bad Ones*. Penguin. Clear, J. (2018).

If you'd like a printable guide to help your practice become more effective, go to: kennedyeffect.com/downloads to print out your free resources.

Accountability

When you tell someone out loud that you are going to do something, you are more compelled to do it. Okay, this is a tough one for most people, including me.

Therefore, tell someone that you are going to start this new habit and ask them to be an accountability partner to keep tabs on whether you are on track or not. I do NOT want to give someone that power to tell me when I missed a deadline or if I ate that candy that one night a week ago. But research tells us that an accountability partner will help you stay on track. You could consider making sure the person you pick is not the type of person that will hold it over your head or someone who is a pushover and will comfort you so you don't feel bad about it.

The goal is NOT to make you feel bad. The goal instead is to help you stay on track. Your accountability partner is someone you trust and someone who has your back. There are many ways to find folks who are trying to do the same thing you are, and they may need an accountability partner to help them. It could be a win-win for you both! For example, join a club where you walk or run and build friendships with folks who are doing what you are doing. You might find someone who needs an accountability partner too. It is a great way to meet new people to boot!

Let me also state that the journal is beneficial because you write down your goals and schedule your new habits in your planner daily. At the end of every day, you fill out the section on reflection.

In the reflection section, you are encouraged to honestly reflect on whether you stayed on track or not. There is no reason to lie to yourself. Be honest. Write it down. Don't make excuses. Just write the real reason. You can use the 5 Whys technique, which can be found by visiting the following link if you find a pattern and are uncertain of the motivation behind your behavior of continuously not following through: www.kennedyeffect.com/downloads

Over time, if you see this repeatedly happening, you will realize that you must decide: is this something I am willing to give up doing? Or is this something I think is important to me, and I want to incorporate it into my life?

If you decide not to move forward, don't judge, don't beat yourself up, but enter a date when you will revisit this decision again tomorrow. Tracking daily makes you really think through the patterns in your life. When you track what you are doing, you can start to see your habits and goals. If you are not tracking your habits, you do not see them. Track them. Be in the minority of folks who achieve their goals. You cannot fix what you cannot measure. Don't hide from your life—live it, by choice. This habit was a choice you made. You said it was important. Follow through.

CHAPTER 13
THE FOUR PILLARS

Are you familiar with the Four Pillars? If you've been soul-searching, you may have encountered them. These four pillars can be used as your guideposts to life.

You may be asking, from where did they come? How and why are they important? And how do they tie into finding meaning?

The origin of the 4 pillars is a blend of the 4 Pillars of Hinduism and Maslow's hierarchy of needs. In the references, I have included two websites that explain more details about each.

For a fulfilled and meaningful life, you must have all four pillars, and all four are intertwined. As you move through the process, you will see where you might be lacking in one or more of these pillars. Do not worry! The daily practice helps you to identify missing elements and then you can take action to resolve them.

Foundation—	Happiness—	Consciousness—	Your True Nature—
What do I need to feel secure?	Are my life's pleasures aligned with my life's purpose?	Being conscious in what you do, say and in how you act	Self-realization, reaching your full potential

Let us start at the bottom—the foundation. Before most people can begin thinking about or devoting time to ponder their purpose in life, they must have a roof over their head, food, and water available and feel a relative amount of safety. If any of these fundamental human needs are not present, it is near-impossible to devote time and thought to these types of questions. Many of us are fortunate to have these basic needs met. However, I would like to share a time when I did not.

When I first began writing this book, I researched available support options because I knew I needed massive help with editing. That is when I realized the financial cost of doing everything required to write the book, such as paying an editor, a graphic designer for the cover, getting it into the proper format for printing, and getting a publicist to help promote the book, and on and on. Also, there is no guarantee that the book will sell enough copies to get my investment back.

Around the same time, I made an appointment to meet with someone to discuss what I needed to have for my retirement. Yes, I realize it is a tactical goal, but it is essential to have something in place to feel secure. I met with a financial advisor and realized I was not ready to retire, and at the rate I was going, I would have to work into my seventies before I could think about retiring. That was a scary day for me. I could not save more money as I was just getting by. I had to make a plan to earn enough income to be able to retire at a reasonable age. So, I went about my life with that worry in the back of my mind thinking that soon (with no particular date in mind, which means I am not going to look at it again for another year or more), I would start saving more money. Then, I went back to focusing on writing this book.

Well, I could not. I tried writing, and I kept procrastinating. The words, thoughts, and ideas were not coalescing. I was not having any success. I implemented the steps to address procrastination. I wrote in my journal that it was my highest priority, my biggest goal. I did all the things that I am encouraging you to do if you run into problems with moving ahead with your goals. What I did and what I learned is what you will hear more of in an upcoming chapter. A little spoiler alert here: I determined that my subconscious was NOT going to let me move forward to write my book when this first foundational pillar was not being met. I did not have security.

Therefore, be mindful of all four pillars. It is my life's purpose to help others with the things I learned about planning and journaling combined and to share those with you. But when a fundamental part of the overall structure is missing, the subconscious will stop you every time. Make sure you have your first pillar—and an answer to the question, "What do I need to feel secure?"

For the next pillar, ask, "Are my life's pleasures aligned with my purpose?"

This pillar assumes you have sat down and fleshed out the questions to determine your mission and goals in life. Most of us have not done this step. As mentioned earlier, we create tactical goals and achieve them (some of us do), but we still feel empty and unfulfilled. Our brains are miraculous and will help to work out answers in that background while we go about our day. Have you ever done that exercise where right before you go to sleep, you tell yourself about a problem you want to solve, and then when you go to sleep and wake up the next morning, you have the answer to the problem? I did that, and it did not work by giving me an answer the next morning, but the next afternoon, when I was walking, the answer came to me. Some believe it is God talking to us, answering our prayers. Researchers say it is how our subconscious works. It will work on that problem in the background, and you will get an answer over time.

The process I share with you uses that type of questioning and goes into it more deeply. You will learn more in that chapter, and I cannot wait to hear feedback on how it might work for you too.

The third pillar is consciousness. Being aware of how you show up, how you act, and your reactions to others are a few examples of the meaning. We have reactions to things, people, and situations all the time. Sometimes, a phrase or action someone takes causes you to feel a certain way.

For example, someone cuts you off in traffic, and you might react negatively. Okay, truth moment here—I have done that more times than I am willing to admit. Through the process of remembering how I want to show up (even when no one is in the car) and this practice, I take a deep breath, count backward from five, and make myself smile. It instantly takes me out of the negative pathway I have forged over the many years of driving in traffic. It works. People are not out to get me by cutting me off in traffic. Someone might just be trying to get home to see their children before bedtime or are late picking up their grandmother. We can never assume the reason for the person taking that action. Maybe they did not see us, or maybe they did and are simply miserable people. It is my reaction that I can control. I choose to be calm and centered and happy. I do not choose to let someone raise my blood pressure over a slight the other person couldn't care less about.

The point is, I choose how I will react. Having control of my emotions is important to my life journey, and I choose to improve my emotional intelligence. That is a technique that helps me to maintain my promise to myself. In fact, according to an article from Pysch Central, "A high EQ helps individuals to communicate better, reduce their anxiety and stress, defuse conflicts, improve relationships, empathize with others, and effectively overcome life's challenges."[1]

Conducting the practice of writing every day and focusing on your goals will help you shore up these pillars. Reflect on your actions daily and ask questions like: Am I staying true to my north star? Are the goals aligned with my pillars? I am not perfect, but I have seen evidence of this daily practice making a positive impact in all areas of my life. I still have a long way to go, but this is a journey, not a destination.

The last pillar is about reaching your full potential as a person. For this pillar, I tend to think about what legacy I want to leave behind when I am reflecting on my life and how I lived. How do I want to be remembered? By conducting this reflection daily, this is where I make sure to connect with people, be kind, make it a point to keep a more positive attitude, be nice to people at the checkout line, etc. I was very patient and calm for a long time, but after I had kids, somehow, the checkout line became my mortal enemy again. The race against time, I guess. This practice has brought me back to realizing there was no reason to be upset about a long line and to show kindness in those moments. I remember to smile.

For the fourth pillar, I can sum it up with this story. I heard a man talking about how he cared for his wife, who had dementia for many years. Someone asked him, "Why do you still go see her every day? She would not know if you were there or not." To which he replied, "Yes, but I would." That is true love, an example of true character, and a role model of how we can all be in life. Doing the right thing when no one is looking is an example of self-actualization. Maslow, whom I have mentioned earlier, says that self-actualization is the highest order of motivations that drive us to reach our true potential. Ultimately, self-actualization is where we always strive to be the best version of ourselves. We are constantly growing as people. If we do not advance, we become stagnate and unfulfilled. Keep growing. What are the four things you need to do each day to ensure you are well-rounded and taking care of yourself?

A word of caution: this is a practice and not an ending point. We are not likely to achieve perfection, but it is something for which we strive. When we stop reaching, we stop growing.

None of these pillars stand alone. They are all related and interconnected. It is important to look at your life and ask yourself the questions related to how you wish to live your life going forward. When you begin your journey, the process will help you to strengthen your life pillars.

---

1. Psych Central, "The Benefits of Emotional Intelligence (EQ) at Work," https://psychcentral.com/blog/the-benefits-of-emotional-intelligence#1

CHAPTER 14
FOUR DAILY ACTIVITIES FOR SUCCESS

We don't fix what we don't measure. Sometimes, we do not like being measured. I certainly do not! But my journal is private and for me. I remind myself that I am worth tracking and spending time investing in my soul. Taking the time out of my day to look at areas where I have an opportunity for growth is fundamental if I wish to have a more fulfilled life. We are always growing as people. If we do not grow, we become stagnate and unfulfilled. Keep growing.

What are the four things you need to do each day to ensure you are well-rounded and taking care of yourself?

- Be clear
- Be grateful
- Be happy
- Be well

These are the four main areas that you will be writing about every day in your journal. You can measure yourself against how well you did every day, add up the score at the end of the week, and then track each week when you review your monthly progress in each category.

I will touch on the four items briefly here in this chapter, and you will see them again in later chapters with more detail provided so you may come to know the significance of these daily elements and how they impact your life.

Be Clear

It is so important to do the work to gain clarity on your vision and mission for your life. Otherwise, those daily goals are tactical and will help you move forward—but not to the level that understanding and planning out goals for your purpose will do.

Once you have completed the worksheet in Chapter 15 on clarity, you can begin planning how you will achieve that vision. It is easy to plan (okay, for me, maybe, but not always for everyone) once you are clear on your goals. I will take you through how to do that in the next few chapters and wanted to touch on a few important points about tasks versus soul goals.

Tasks are the items I described earlier about saving for a vacation, the work you need to put in to get a degree, etc. They are tactical and are unrelated to your soul goals. For example, picking up the dry cleaning, shopping for food, etc., are daily activities you need to conduct to live your life. Soul goals are tasks as well, but they are tied to your vision.

Soul goals are actually tasks as well, but they are tied to your vision. When you start out each day focusing on exactly what the tasks are that you need to accomplish to reach your full potential, then you remember to do them each day. For example, a similar vision to mine is to help people achieve their life's purpose. The daily goal that is tied to that vision might be, "Call my sister and coach her through the issue she is having around her business goals." My calendar might be filled up with appointments, meetings, and things I need to do for work, but if it was a random call from my sister asking for help, I would not add it to the calendar and would help her at that moment, of course. However, if she told me that she wanted help with a particular business issue, I would add time to my schedule to reach out to my sister for that conversation. Adding a soul goal as a planned activity on my calendar helps me remember actions I accomplished that helped me move my mission forward.

Hopefully, this example helps to differentiate this idea of task versus soul goals. If I did not place any tasks for the day toward reaching my soul goals, how would I know I achieved them? The fact is that I would not likely know. When you reflect on the week and all the things you have accomplished, it is helpful to refer to your calendar to remember all the things you have completed. If we leave it to memory, we might only remember the things that went wrong instead of the things you did that contributed toward your soul goals.

Here is another example. Let's say that my vision is still the same, but I was not finished writing my book. I would enter an amount of time into my calendar for writing my book. I am dedicated to reaching my life's purpose, and I would block out two-hour time slots from 6:30 a.m. to 8:30 a.m. and switch over to my day job afterward. Sometimes, I would do another one-hour or two-hour block in the evening to ensure I stayed on track. The reason I am so dedicated to completing this work and willing to work overtime to make it happen is that it is in alignment with my life's purpose. Without a clear purpose, I am not this dedicated to things other than my family. When you are crystal clear on your life's purpose, the tasks are clear, and for me, it drives a fire in my belly to get those purpose-related tasks completed.

We will talk more about these topics in planning, but I wanted to make sure you knew this was the first of four aspects of your life you will need to make sure you include every day.

Be Grateful

I have covered quite a bit about the research behind gratitude. Being grateful fills your soul and gets you out of yourself to feel love and compassion in your heart. Be grateful for who you are, what you have, where you are in life, and for those who are in your life.

Take up as much space as needed to write down reasons you are grateful for daily. I like to do this upon waking and always think of my dog, who is so excited to see me come down the stairs in the morning. Even if I do not feel joy at that moment, his antics and happiness help me remember to feel it. So, I thank God for that dog every single day. What a faithful friend!

Gratitude is a needle-mover—just do it!

Be Happy

Time for a reality check. We cannot always just flip a switch and make ourselves happy. There are tragic events in our lives that cause such deep pain and anguish, and that is not the time to try to make yourself happy. Nor can you snap out of mental illness with a smile. I am referring to the times when you are in a checkout line and the cashier is new, and you just watched the person training the new cashier walk away to help someone else. Then, you watch the line slow down even more. That is a great time to remember that we were all new at something at some point in our lives, too. How about giving the new cashier a chance and exercising patience on your part? Even if you are frustrated because it is taking longer than you think it should, it is in those moments that we can remember to simply smile. The simple act of smiling actually changes us internally, and, according to the University of Pittsburgh, "choosing to smile and making yourself lift the corners of your mouth upwards activates the release of hormones like dopamine and endorphins, which can make you feel better and combat stress." [1]

Be Well

In order to be able to have a fulfilled life, it is important to be as well as you can be. It is akin to what they tell you on an airplane—you must put on your oxygen mask before you can help others. If you are not taking care of yourself, you cannot be at your best for any length of time. Listed below are the three aspects most would agree are what is required on a daily basis to improve and maintain health: 1. Move Well, 2. Eat Well, 3. Sleep Well.

Move Well

When I was in college, I participated in an exercise research program where the premise was to show that exercise improved the mind. We were asked to sit on a computer and take a test to assess our level of mental acuity and reaction time. Then, we were placed on a treadmill for a certain amount of time and asked to re-take the test. What they found was that everyone scored higher on the test AFTER they ran on the treadmill. The second test was not the same as the first but was an equally challenging type of test. I believe they switched other groups of folks to take the second test first and the first one second as well to ensure accuracy. An interesting side note: those people who had reported experiencing a runner's high had the highest scores of all the participants.

The point here is that we are meant to get up and move around. We are not meant to sit in front of laptops all day as we work. We do not get the same type of blood circulation as when we walk and are active throughout the day versus sitting at a desk. Therefore, moving our bodies is essential to improve our minds and health. When we move our bodies, we can think more clearly, and our bodies can do the things they need to keep us healthy.

Eat Well

Have you heard of an overweight person who is literally starving? I would not have believed it until I started tracking my food intake in a phone app called Chronometer. It is free and it is accurate in terms of the nutritional value found in the foods I eat on a daily basis. Chronometer, like many other free apps, allows a person to enter all the food they are eating and in what amounts. At the end of the day, it calculates the number of calories, amount of fats, fiber, and nutrients your body needs every day to sustain health. The problem is that most people are not interested in entering everything they are eating. I entered everything I ate, the accurate weight of the food, and serving amounts because I was on a diet and had not lost any weight. What was shown back to me every day was that I was eating a few hundred calories more each day than what I was burning, and therefore was overeating. But more importantly, I realized that I was not getting enough of the required daily amounts of important nutrients. I was not feeding my body enough fuel to maintain health. I was completely shocked! I started working with a dietician, and together, we worked out a better food plan that would allow me to lose weight slowly as well as feed my body the right nutrients in the right amounts to ensure I was getting the minimum daily requirements we all need to maintain health.

Chronometer is free, but there are many other free apps you can download and use to track your daily eating habits. I thought I was getting enough calcium, but I was not getting anywhere near enough. I had been eating like that for years. I am grateful to have learned early enough that I can make changes so the long-term impact is (hopefully) not that dire. Some women do not have enough calcium in their bones when they get older and are at risk of easily breaking their bones as they age. I do not want to be in that category and am grateful to have been able to make the changes to avoid that outcome in the future.

I was slightly overweight AND not getting enough nutrients. Not a great combination. I would encourage everyone to track what they eat to ensure they are getting enough of the right foods that help us maintain our well-being.

The bottom line is that the foods we eat are important to our health, and if we do not fuel our bodies with the right nutrients, the long-term outcome is not as great as it could be. Long story short: eat your veggies!

Sleep Well

Sleep is vital to your well-being. According to Harvard University, "sleep and mental health are closely connected. Sleep deprivation affects your psychological state and mental health." [2]

In fact, lack of sleep can increase your risk of diabetes, high blood pressure, impact memory, and can even cause weight gain! Sleep is foundational to good health. We cannot be healthy if we aren't getting enough rest at night.

Also, sleep affects the levels of a hormone called leptin that signals to your brain that you are full. This hormone decreases over time due to lack of sleep. But it also increases another hormone called ghrelin that makes you want to eat more. It is a double whammy! You might find yourself sneaking to the fridge for a snack when you've just recently eaten a meal and are not truly hungry. Make sure you are getting enough sleep.

I have trouble sleeping at times and have taken steps to follow a routine that is suggested by many people to ensure I have the best opportunity of getting a good night's sleep.

First, block the light from outside with blackout curtains, if possible. Then, look for lights in your room that do not go out like your clock (I turn mine to face the other direction). I realized that my air conditioner control panel remains lit at night as well; I now cover it and unplug any other unnecessary light sources so my room is in total darkness. It is recommended that you shut down all electronic devices at least an hour before bedtime.

The reason is due to the light signaling to your body that it is daytime still. It interferes with the body's natural production of melatonin. Melatonin is a hormone our bodies naturally produce that regulates our sleep. We need to be on a regular sleep cycle for our bodies to release all the right hormones and go into a relaxing and restful good night's sleep.

There are blue light glasses available—much more commonly now—that can be worn to watch tv or if you must be on your phone or computer in the evening. Conventional wisdom suggests you shut down all electronics and read a book or conduct something relaxing to wind down before bedtime.

During the day, get outside and get some sun. Sunlight signals your body to produce serotonin, which is another hormone that helps you feel calm and focused (no wonder so many people love sunbathing). It also helps to regulate your circadian rhythm, which helps you stay awake during the day and asleep at night.

Other important sleep advice is to avoid long naps during the day or naps that are after 3 p.m., as napping might interfere with your ability to fall asleep at your regular time. Also, staying away from caffeine in the afternoon/evening is a helpful step to take since caffeine keeps some of us awake even when we might be sleepy.

Getting regular exercise helps us sleep better too. Just do not exercise within three hours of bedtime because your body releases endorphins when exercising. Endorphins are energizing, which is excellent, but not when it is time for rest. Endorphins also make us feel good, which is why some people are addicted to exercise. I am working on making myself addicted to exercise, albeit in a healthy manner. Apparently, the more active you are, the more you wear yourself out, and then your body gladly repairs itself during sleep. There is yet another reason to exercise regularly!

To summarize, taking care of yourself first by placing that oxygen mask on your face before helping others is incredibly important to maintain overall wellness. We want to be the best we can be, whether we are working toward our goals or just spending time with family and friends. Having the fundamentals of good eating habits, a daily exercise regimen, and a solid block of seven to eight hours of sleep each night will help ensure that you have a healthy mind and body so you can then feed your soul.

And remember to celebrate your wins. Remember that YOU did it!

---

1. Supporting Our Valued Adolescents (SOVA), University of Pittsburgh, "The Act of Smiling," https://sova.pitt.edu/be-positive-the-act-of-smiling
2. Harvard Health Publishing, "Sleep and mental health: Sleep deprivation can affect your mental health." https://www.health.harvard.edu/newsletter_article/sleep-and-mental-health

CHAPTER 15
GETTING CLEAR

How do you get clear on what you want your life to be?

It will take time. I wanted to set expectations because clarity does not always magically show up for many people. There are some who already know they want to be an artist, a musician, a doctor, and other careers. But some of us do not have any idea about what our passions are or have not come close to determining our life's purpose. I was there. I know what it feels like. I made do with my career and truly do enjoy the work that I do. But there is something more, and I am grateful to have found it and want to help you find yours too.

Find that thing that you are passionate about, that lights you up, and get into it in whatever way makes the most sense for you. For whatever it is that you love, there are many avenues that relate to that passion. Then, pursue it in a way that can make a difference in your life.

Being passionate about your animal brings a tremendous amount of joy. It has for me. And as I reflect on all the other things that bring me joy, I realize that there are other areas where I am passionate as well. I love learning, for example. Learning something new every day helps light me up and brings joy. Musicians find passion and meaning in the music they create. I find I am passionate about painting and am okay with using the art of expression after work or on weekends to create. It is not as important to me that I perfect it as much as use it as a form of expression that I enjoy. You might have similar things about which you are passionate but find that there is still more you seek.

That is where I found an approach that helped me, and I wish to share it with you. Let me start by saying, "congratulations!" Seriously, congratulations for being in the minority of people who take the time to sit down and think about this topic. For those of you who already have a goal, I encourage you to follow along in this process as well.

Life evolves and changes, and so do we. Continually coming back to this practice is important because you may outgrow what you thought your life purpose was. Maybe you got good enough at something and are seeking something more fulfilling at this next stage in your life. Whatever the reason, checking in with this practice will help you continually question and become aware of your life's purpose and will keep you on track to achieve the goals you set.

What if I do not know what I am passionate about?

What I suggest people do when they are not clear on their passions, is to do some soul-searching homework.

1. Write a list of things about which you are passionate. Do you like volunteering at animal shelters? Love music?
2. What do you spend your free time doing? Make a list. Do you read books; if so, what kind? Movies, documentaries, cooking, food, gardening, hiking, exercising, list them all.

3. What are you naturally good at? I'm naturally good at helping groups organize and take action quickly. Are you great at hosting parties, baseball, whatever it is? Write down what comes to mind. Make a list.

4. Ask trusted friends and peers what they think you are naturally good at doing. Compile the list.

5. Write a list of your accomplishments. Work, high school, sports, etc. List as many as you can.

6. List your top five values. These are important to determine because these values are your true north star. They should guide any decisions you make about your life and career, and they will help you stay the course. You can easily conduct an online search to get a list of values to get you started. The difficult part is narrowing the list.

7. List all the things, activities, and experiences that bring you joy.

8. Review all the answers, categorize them, and look for themes.

Taking the time and investing in yourself to do this homework and figure out what makes you tick will help you get clear on creating the life you want. When you review all the items you have written down, you will start seeing emerging themes. For example, one client realized she was passionate about the environment and spent a lot of time reading, learning, volunteering, and supporting various environmental causes important to her. As she thought more deeply about the emerging themes, she realized she could take her passion and bring it to work by organizing volunteer activities and partnering with external not-for-profits to help make a difference. In fact, that became her mission: to make a difference in the world by leaving it better than she found it. Eventually, she was able to get a director-level role in a not-for-profit and is living her mission.

You can also take a strengths-finder test. There is a strengths-finder test through the Clifton Strengths Finder, which at the time of this writing costs roughly $90. But there is also a free version that gives you more information than simply your strengths, called 16personalities, about which I will share more details next following the Clifton Strengths Finder information.

Clifton Strengths Finder is an assessment tool that Gallup has bought. It is an assessment whose results help you understand things you are naturally good at doing. Then, it helps you learn how to develop your greatest talents. According to the website. Don Clifton developed the assessment and wrote about it in his book *Now, Discover Your Strengths*. The guidance from the author of the assessment suggests you focus on those strengths and develop them. [1]

I will go into more depth about a Yale course on happiness that encourages you to know your strengths; research does show that if you do those things that come naturally to you, you will be happier. One thing I would say is that it is also important to know your weaknesses and bolster those areas as needed. In other words, if you are a project manager and are good at planning but not so good at task management, then to be successful as a project manager, you need to build up those task management skills to do your job effectively.

Learning your strengths is always a great thing as it helps you to know more about yourself and what makes you tick. For people who are not sure about their passions, knowing your strengths gives you a head start to begin thinking about roles suited to those strengths.

The other test is called https://www.16personalities.com/ [2]
16 Personalities and is free. It gives you a more robust personality assessment, including your strengths. It does not go to the level of granularity that the Clifton assessment does, but it does give you a solid idea of things you are good at, tells you famous

people who have your traits, and suggests jobs that might fit your overall profile.

Their personality model "…incorporates the latest advances in psychometric research, combining time-tested concepts with robust and highly accurate testing techniques." The website's authors also have an article about the validity of the tests. One or both of those assessments will get you down the path and help you develop potential roles that might suit you.

But if you find you are really good in a particular area, exploring something that plays to those strengths may help you take a step toward learning about your passion.

Growth

"I have no special talent. I am only passionately curious."
  —Albert Einstein

Yes, it makes sense that people are most happy when they do work that plays to their strengths. Let me also mention that we are humans, and as such, if we do not continue growing and learning, we become stagnate. We will become unfulfilled. We can learn to look at those jobs or roles we want to step into and think about both strengths and weaknesses. Like the example above, if you decide your life's purpose is to be a business owner but you do not like keeping the books, you'd be best served to ramp up your book-keeping skills so that you could oversee the work and understand if someone were funneling money out of your business. You could hire someone to do the job you do not like to do, but you MUST know enough to oversee the work so you do not get taken advantage of.

Remember, relying solely on your strengths likely won't take you all the way forward to your perfect job, but knowing what they are will help you take steps toward determining your life's purpose.

To live a more fulfilled life, you must always make room to grow!

The great thing about learning is that it expands your mind. Remember to look back and track all the things you have learned on your journey in your journal. You will be amazed at all the things you have learned!

"The beautiful thing about learning is nobody can take it away from you."

—B. B. King

If you are just starting out in your career and are not certain the direction to take, consider taking one step. It is so easy to fall into analysis paralysis. That means that you spend all your time thinking, planning, and contemplating that you end up not doing anything.

Taking the first step into anything helps. When you move into a new role, it expands your mind. For example, you might go into the restaurant industry to try cooking because you dream of opening your own restaurant one day. Some people ruminate over getting a loan and think about leasing a building when they could simply go work at one first. Let's say you find a restaurant you really like and apply for a job there. Okay, so you might have to be a hostess and then move into waiting on tables first. These roles give you perspective on how the restaurant runs, how customers' needs get met, how to provide customer service (to make sure you get good tips!), and more. Over time, you convince the owner to let you work in the kitchen. Maybe you become a prep chef. As time goes on, you learn more and more about the restaurant and all the stress and types of management that must be done to run a good restaurant. That experience likely would set you up very well to run your own restaurant one day. But let's say you realize it is not enjoyable. What's next? Was that time wasted? Well, you might come back and use the tools in this book, and you are still interested in being in the restaurant industry. Let us say you met the baker, who delivers the wonderful desserts the restaurant serves, and she mentions she has an opening for a baker. Let's say you always loved baking with your mom and have wonderful memories of those activities, so you give it a shot.

Here in this new role, you learn all the ins and outs of baking but realize after some time that this is interesting work, and it was fun to try, but you want something more. Now what?

In your journaling and tracking of all you have been learning, you realize just how much you have learned about running a restaurant and now a bakery. You have learned about ordering supplies, customer service, and maybe even the financial aspects. You saw how hard it is to find good help, techniques used to keep employees happy, and even what types of customers the different businesses attract.

You might then take that knowledge and start a food supply business or a staffing firm that focuses on the food industry. There will likely be a lot of new doors that will open to you because you now have this broad experience. The bottom line is that unless you start, you will never grow.

The same thing applies to musicians. Let's say you love playing guitar. You form a band, practice at night, and get a few gigs at local bars but realize you are not that passionate about trying to make a living as a musician. What you might learn is that you love simply playing guitar and continue doing it as a hobby. Or you might find you love teaching music or even being the manager of a music band. The point is that it can lead to other jobs that you do love. It's all about taking that first step.

The Montessori method is similar in that it allows a child to explore their interests in full until they get bored. So, if you really love birds, for example, they will provide you with books on birds, bird puzzles, math related to birds, and so on. You pick a new subject when you get bored, and they keep teaching that way. They still teach the fundamentals, but the point is that they help children learn by following their passions. Taking that career step is similar. It will lead you to places you could not even imagine when you first started out.

Let's discuss my overall system so you can see how it is structured. It is basically:

1. Know the game in which you find yourself
2. Realize how the game is stacked against you
3. Create your own rules
4. Find your life's purpose/mission.
5. Determine how you attain your life's mission.
6. Figure out what steps you need to take to get there. These steps are your goals.

With that being said, let's start on the system for figuring out some things about which you are passionate.

Get out a piece of paper and start writing the things you believe are your purpose. You might start out with 20 different things, and as you keep following the process, you get crystal clear. Maybe you write something like: "I want to make others happy" or "I want to help people." Some people start out that simply and then add to it or change their list completely. The simple act of starting sets you on the journey. For most, it does not come overnight; it takes journaling, thinking about it, sleeping on it, and just trying it out. Daily journaling will distill this down for you. It will come. As Dory says in the movie *Finding Nemo*, "Just keep swimming." (DeGeneres, *Finding Nemo, 2003*)

Why do you want this goal, this thing, this lifestyle? Why is it important to you? Then, ask yourself again. Once you have that new answer, ask, "why?" for that next new answer. Do this 5-10 times. It is called the 5 Whys. (Please visit kennedyeffect.-com/downloads for more information.)

START AGAIN. Then, go back to step 1 with your new goal each day. Write it on your weekly tracker in the top left. Every day, rinse and repeat. Over time, you will see patterns of the ones that truly resonate in your daily life. Now you know your goals for life, but more importantly, you know the "why." I am providing a graphic, "The 5 Whys," below for easy reference. Circle the final statement once you've gotten to the end, rewrite it across the top or bottom, and then circle it for clarity on where you landed. Write that statement in your daily planner each day. if you don't use a daily planner, write the statement and place it somewhere visible to you throughout the day. This practice will help you stay focused. Do this all over again when it does not feel right or no longer fits. Keep in mind that as you get started, things will change, improve, and refine over time. It is important to do this exercise periodically in your life. It helps you connect to your soul because your mission will change as you evolve. The more you connect, the more aware you are of what is important to you at that moment in time.

Keep in mind that as you get started, things will change and improve and get refined. It is important to do this exercise periodically in your life. It helps you to connect to your soul because as you evolve, your mission will change. The more you connect, the more aware you are of what is important to you at that moment in time.

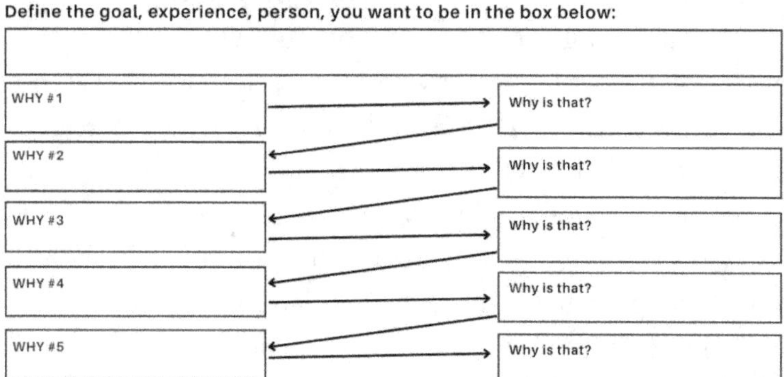

You might have trouble at the beginning, but just keep writing and writing and questioning and questioning. The 5 Whys are used in design thinking (a process for solving problems by prioritizing the consumer's needs above all else) to help the software engineers gain clarity on solving problems in the software they are creating for end users. It was developed in Lean Six Sigma (a data-driven method for improving, optimizing and stabilizing business and manufacturing processes) to identify root causes of systems or processes that were broken. It is also used in project management to get a deeper understanding of the purpose of the project and/or initiatives.

Here is a great example from a LinkedIn article:

Scenario – The Parking Ticket

A college student has arrived late to the team meeting, explaining it is not their fault but that they are late because of a parking ticket. A few questions are asked about the ticket, and it turns out the parking ticket was a consequence of other actions, not the cause.

Q1. Why did you get a parking ticket?
A. I parked in a spot I was not meant to be in.

Q2. Why?
A. I was running late, so parked there to get to a meeting on time.

Q3. Why?
A. I got up late.

Q4. Why?
A. The alarm did not go off.

Q5. Why?
A: I stayed up late to watch a film and I forgot to set it.[3]

You can see it took several times to get to the root cause of why the student was late. Our brains are very accustomed to working in the manner of keeping things superficial and finding the easiest first answer. We too need to dig in more deeply to keep questioning ourselves as to the reason we want a certain thing.

Now, let us break this down for how it might show up when you resist a habit that you know is good for you.

PROBLEM: I cannot get up early enough to do my workout in the morning.

Q1. Why?
A1. I am too tired and need sleep.

Q2. Why?
A2. I go to bed too late at night.

Q3. Why?

A3. I end up working late at night to get my deliverables submitted on time.

Q4. Why?
A4. I like to play with the dog in the afternoon for at least an hour to make sure he gets exercise.

Q5. Why?
A5. Because I feel the need to exercise too.

That was enlightening! What if this person would get up in the morning to exercise and then later in the day take a few different 15-minute breaks to take the dog out and get some fresh air rather than spending an entire hour all at once? This would free him or her up to have a more relaxing evening and get to bed at a reasonable hour.

Here is another example where you might see the core reason for feeling anxious or when you want to go for that cigarette. Let's take a look:

PROBLEM: I feel anxious right now, and I can't calm down to go to sleep.

Q1. Why?
A1. Things at work are stressing me out.

Q2. Why?
A2. There is a job posting I want to apply for, but I can't seem to decide if it is the right move for me.

Q3. Why?
A3. What if it turns out to be something I am not good at or I don't like the boss? Then I am stuck.

Q4. What's wrong with getting stuck?
A4. I have gone for a job in the past that I did get, but it wasn't right for me, and I don't want to make another mistake again.

Q5. Why don't you want to make another mistake again?
A5. Because thinking about being in another job where I am unhappy is causing me to be stressed.

In this case, you could keep going further and ask more questions to dig more deeply.

Q6. What steps can you take to ensure you will be happy in your next job?
A6. I could meet with the hiring manager and their direct reports to get more information about the role before I apply. That way I have a deeper understanding of what is involved.

Voila! The art of digging deeper is important in all of our life decisions. It helps us to get very clear on the reasons we may be feeling a certain way. If you feel anxious or some feeling and cannot get more granular, pull out the feelings wheel and identify which feeling you are or were feeling. It may help you to better identify a specific type of anxious feeling, which may shed more light on your current scenario. In the case above, the person was clear he was feeling anxious and got to a conclusion rather easily.

Let's say someone felt anxious, and if they check the feelings wheel, they might identify that anxiety stems from fear, but that answer does not seem to shed more light on their circumstance. They look further on the wheel and identify that they feel over-whelmed. Then, upon more reflection, that person realizes they were picking up the load from a co-worker who took maternity leave and had just recently gotten a promotion. The combination of events can be overwhelming at times. This person can then figure out a strategy that might help them offload some work to another person so they do not feel overwhelmed. More about the Feelings Wheel can be found in Chapter 23 on Fear.

Our minds are constantly running on autopilot, letting us know when something is wrong through our feelings. It is important to pay attention to our feelings and to sit down and ask the 5 Whys to get to the root cause. This method works!

Many of us have taught ourselves to go to the candy jar in moments like those described above to self-soothe. Or we may turn to that drink or another habit that is not serving us. Implementing the 5 Whys technique makes it possible to get to the root cause of what is truly bothering you. Once you become aware, you can take steps to mitigate (or at least express) your feelings if the situation cannot be changed. Journaling in that instance is helpful to pull forth your thoughts about the subject and to give your mind a rest. You can come back to it later, and maybe a solution will come to you. The act of writing it down, as mentioned before, will help with the stressful feelings.

In addition, when you ask the 5 Whys in relation to your Life's Purpose questions, the answer may not be made clear right away. Keep asking until you cannot move further in the questioning process. Walk away. Take a long walk, a relaxing bath, or do something that will make you relax and give your mind time to think. Your subconscious will be working in the background to come up with an answer. Later, your inner voice might give you an idea. The voice might be small, and you might automatically shut it down as being silly or say, "I can't do that!" Take a minute and listen to the voice. It might be the answer you need to hear, and the right next step to something that will help you along.

Let's say you have chosen "I want to help people" as your life's purpose. Then you start asking the 5 Whys. It might go something like this:

Q1. Why?
A1. Because it is the right thing to do.

Q2. Why?
A2. Because my parents always taught me to be nice to people.

Q3. Why?
A3. Because you reap what you sow and being nice to people is a choice I make.

Q4. Why?
A4. Because I want people to be nice to me.

Q5. Why?
A5. Because I want to get along with people.

Q6. Why?
A6. Because I am lonely and want to connect more with others.

This deeper answer is a big one! We may have aspirations to help other people because that was what we were taught. But when a person has this feeling that they are unfulfilled and provide a simple answer without further questioning to get to the core of what it is they truly want, they might miss the mark entirely. Let's face it—if this person went ahead and started showing random acts of kindness, they would connect more with other people, and the net result would be the same. It is important to really understand your drivers because it can lead to better decision-making, and you truly attain more self-awareness by following this model. You would not be blindly showing random acts of kindness, but you would be very intentional in showing kindness, and in that act, connect more deeply to the person to whom you are being kind.

The 5 Whys is a great tool to have in your toolkit as you navigate life. It can apply to almost any problem, it does not take long to accomplish, and it might just help you find the answer to your life's purpose, and even then, bring more clarity around it.

This process will set you up for success in designing a life you are not only proud of but can help you find your life's purpose.

---

1. Gallup, Clifton Strengths, https://www.gallup.com/cliftonstrengths/en/252137/home.aspx
2. Sixteen personalities, https://www.16personalities.com/
3. LinkedIn, "The BA Skill Set—The Five Whys Technique," https://www.linkedin.com/pulse/ba-skill-set-5-whys-technique-jon-derbyshire/

CHAPTER 16

BREAK DOWN PLANS INTO MANAGEABLE PIECES OF WORK

Many of my clients come to me overwhelmed and wishing they had more time in their day. One of the most practical tips I can share to alleviate that feeling and to bring more order into their lives is to take time up front to organize things so that they are more manageable.

Breaking down a plan into manageable action steps is where some of us get stuck. Sometimes, we look at that huge plan (or, in my case, my messy closet) and just walk away, overwhelmed by the thought of getting it all completed. I know I do every time I look in my closet!

But what if I were able to say to myself, "Okay, I will start on the upper shelf of my closet and only work on the right side. I will pull all those items down, sort them, throw away what I no longer need, and neatly stack the items I wish to keep." That is a manageable way to look at the problem of the messy closet. The next Saturday, I can do the left side. I might even realize I can do two shelves at a time. I might suddenly find that I am done, with a nicely cleaned closet and no more anxiety.

We can chunk work down into manageable pieces so we can

get tasks done within our busy schedules. Let's go back to the book-writing example again. When I first thought about writing a book, I was so excited. I was thinking about all these ideas I had that I could share to help people find their life's purpose, and I couldn't WAIT to get started.

I blocked off my first Saturday morning to focus on sitting down at the computer with my coffee in hand and started typing away. Then, reality kicked in. What was I thinking? I don't know how to write! Where do I start? How could I have ever thought that I could write a book anyway? All my fears, doubts, and anxiety kicked into full gear, and I froze. I did not know where to start.

Many of our ideas never come to fruition because we allow fears, doubts, and concerns about what others will say to take over and stop us from moving forward. In this instance, I had my worksheet, where I said my mission was to help people. My goal was to write this book. And as I re-read the writing on those pages (yes, I needed more than one to get super clear on what I wanted to do and the reason why), I remembered my "why."

I ended up persevering through all the doubts—I still have them as I write this book—and I keep going because I taped my worksheet on my wall and look at it every time I get stuck with writing. It motivates me to keep moving. I know why I wanted to do this, and I know it will help at least one person in the process. If there are more, it is a bonus.

When you know the reason behind your goals, you tend to have a higher success rate in achieving them.

That leads me to the next important factor to achieving your goals: you MUST visit them daily.

I suggest you use some type of planner that contains elements that help you periodically evaluate your life's purpose so you remain on track and understand your intention. It also combines your goals and the steps you are taking every day to achieve them. Then, you combine that with journaling and the other elements contained within the journal, and you are revisiting your reason why and the steps you are taking to get there every single day. This daily habit leads to your success. Please visit my website for a sheet you can print out with elements that will help you focus and stay on track at www.kennedyeffect.com/downloads.

I thought about my book day and night, night and day, while on walks, while working out, etc. I shared what I was doing with friends. I was obsessed! Defining my purpose, getting clear on my goals, and working on my daily habits got me here. You are reading this book! But this was not just me—this is what successful people do. When interviewed, they were crystal clear on their purpose and obsessively created daily goals and worked toward them. So, use the planning page found on my website or your planner of choice to track these elements. My planner is designed for this process and people like you who wish to achieve their goals in life.

There is one more thing…

If you want success in achieving your goals, you must possess the discipline to do this every day. That is why it is so important to form the habits that help you move toward your goals and not away from them. It is important that you show up every day and plan for your day ahead. Then, at night, track what you did during the day to move the needle forward on reaching your goals.

When you journal daily about your intention, track the goals that will help you get there, and consistently show up and focus on those tasks that will help you get to your goal, then you have a tremendous and powerful ability to achieve what you set out to do. This is exciting stuff! It seems easy but it is not. Again, most people do not know how to uncover their "why" in life. Please, share this book with them and help them to move forward in their lives, too. Pay it forward.

I get so excited thinking about these steps for success and how it simply works.

You need to be realistic about your goals. If you said your goal is to get money so you can buy a big house, that is not exactly a strong intention. If you said you intended to make money so you could buy your first house to provide stability for your children, then that is an intention that most would agree would stick. Remember to check your intentions so that they are meaningful.

Okay, now you have your big goal. What's next? Write it down. Research by Dr. Gail Matthews, Psychology Professor at the Dominican University of California, shows you are 42% more likely to achieve your goal if you write it down. Not type it—write it. There is a mind-body-brain connection there too. [1]

But what if the goal is huge? It's so big, and there are so many parts involved. It is at this point that most people walk away. They drop their dreams on the ground. Don't do that! Let's break it down first!

Create workstreams. Let's say you want to save the world. Admirable goal. But when you step back and think about all the things that it would take, well, you dream about it and then shelve the idea. Another goal could be to recycle and contribute to saving the world.

You might think, *Great! Well, the oceans are vast and huge, and the earth is so big. Where do I start?*

Okay, what about a local lake or local park? What if I start there? Well, that local park has a lake and land. What if I created two workstreams and recruited volunteers with boats to help clean the lake and another workstream of volunteers to walk the park and pick up plastic to recycle? That sounds great.

Well, now we have all the plastic; what's next? I need another workstream to get the plastic to the recycling center.

Now you can take steps that will be needed to accomplish each workstream.

Steps needed in each workstream:

- I need to tell people
- I need a way for them to sign up
- I need to know who wants to help in which workstream

And you write the steps. It is simple! Now, ask yourself, "How do I track it all?" and "What might prevent me from achieving my goal?" Research shows if you identify your hurdles up front, you then figure out a way to mitigate them. So, when your hurdles show up, guess what? You already have a plan to resolve them up front.

Write down a list of things that might prevent you from moving forward. You might notice you are not moving forward and sticking with your goals. It is important to write down the things that come to mind when you actually sit down and try to move forward. Often, it is self-doubt and fear that prevents us from moving forward. Please refer to the chapter on Fear, Chapter 23, for more information. In addition, using the 5 Whys here can be beneficial to help pull out the root cause of what is stopping you from moving forward.

Let's look at a good example of risk mitigation that conveys the idea more fully; say that you are planning for an outdoor celebration. One of the first things to consider when thinking about a venue is to ask yourself what would happen if it rained. Does the venue have inside space that also can be reserved in the event of inclement weather?

Many of us automatically plan for the happy path only and not for potential pitfalls. For example, I had an important presentation recently where I needed to sell an idea to senior leadership. I had the happy path laid out; I just needed to tell them about the idea and how it would help the company. But in the planning, I also made sure I played devil's advocate by thinking of different opinions someone might say during the presentation if they were questioning the idea or were exploring other areas around it. I put myself into the shoes of each leader present and thought about this idea from their perspective. It helped me to be ready and more prepared for alternative viewpoints so I would not be thrown off in the meeting.

I also thought about what I would do if someone said, "That is a stupid idea!" Now, that response was not likely to happen, but thinking about it in advance helped prepare me more thoroughly for an out-of-the-box-type question someone might have. I practiced answering the questions in advance so that it became natural. I came up with a response that I have seen several people use in the past: "Tell me more…"

Being prepared for the risks that may or may not occur will help you navigate your goals much more smoothly.

Another technique that helps in those situations is to take three deep breaths. You do not have to respond right away. Take that time to get centered and count backward from five. The act of counting backward takes your mind away from fear and self-doubt. This simple technique might help you if you ever find yourself in a similar situation.

The last essential item to mention around your goals is to Celebrate! Plan for this. To comply with the 4 Pillars, you must take the time and remember to ENJOY your life. Remember to reward yourself. Take the time to reflect, celebrate, and relish in what you accomplished. It will motivate you with your future goals.

Keep your goal sheet close by and refer to it often. Just like all of the things I am suggesting, they are important windows into your life's purpose. Take the time to write them down and pick them apart with the 5 Whys again to ensure they are still accurate. Having all the work you did to arrive at YOUR goals is important to have on hand to refer to when the going gets more difficult.

Okay, now you have made an entire list of goals that you wish to accomplish to meet your mission. Now what?

Prioritization

Start to put numbers on the goals. Number one being the most important and number and ten being the least. Start with the goals that are a top priority for you. If you have trouble deciding which ones are most important, think about which of them will move you forward the fastest with the most impact. Those are the ones you might decide are the first to be accomplished. There might also be goals you must do first (and it may not be one you actually are too fond of) because it needs to be accomplished before you can move onto other goals that will really move the needle. Think through those scenarios as well; it is important not to ignore the goals we do not like as much since this may slow us down in the long run.

Now, look at the top goals. Can you do them all simultaneously? Most likely you cannot. What helps now is to start thinking about the tasks that you need to accomplish to reach the goal(s). For example, in the case of that big event we were planning for earlier, the tasks might be:

1. Identify the stakeholder (the person paying for the event). Meet with them to ensure their celebration ideas are captured.
2. Capture the goal of the event.
3. Agree on the budget and venue type.
4. Agree on the entertainment and food/drink.
5. Create top 2-3 venues with budget considerations and present them to your stakeholder.
6. Ensure each venue has rain or shine contingencies.
7. Book venue.
8. Print invitations.
9. Etc.

Then, do this for your top few goals. You might find that you can conduct both goals simultaneously because they have similar outcomes. Maybe you are starting your own professional event-planning business, and along with this celebration affair, you are also planning a wedding and can check dates for both events with the venues. You get the idea. Then those would be two work-streams that can be conducted simultaneously.

Next, begin adding the tasks to your planner. Figure out the end date and work backward to determine when certain things need to be completed. For example, in book-writing, you may have committed to releasing the book by a certain date, and you need to work backward to understand timelines of when you must have the book finished to be on time.

In the ideal planner, it would have a monthly goals view that you would use to enter dates for the upcoming month. Then, you would look at the upcoming week and list out the tasks you need to accomplish for that week that need to be carried out in order to reach your monthly goals.

But who does that with our own goals? For example, most people will enter all their work and personal goals into their work calendar so that there is one place to track all their activities. The problem is that they do not journal about things on their calendar every day. They are not physically writing down their "why" and therefore are not tracking the things they completed toward their "why." That is why I encourage you to use a tracker that captures your work and personal activities and has a place for your mission. When you see it and write it out daily, it becomes at the forefront of everything you do. There is something tangibly satis-fying when you can look at your list of tasks and see all the things you completed, especially when those tasks are moving you closer to your mission. Electronic is not the same as handwritten. Again, look at the science.

You have taken the big goal and have now broken it out into manageable tasks that are on your planner. You can see the big items you need to accomplish on your monthly calendar, and you can see what is important to accomplish for the upcoming week.

Last, you have outlined each day what tasks are going to move you forward to reach your goals. More importantly, every single day, you connect to your "why." Your mission is what is driving you to reach those goals. Your mission is your promise to yourself that you make and refer to every single day to reach your goals.

Having a journal where you write down and think about your plan helps you to focus more clearly on the goals you MUST achieve to hit your mission. I make it easy for you on the planner page I reference on my website, but you can go to your local discount store and buy a notebook, too. Just write down your goals and remember to add your answers to why you are grateful every day and other items discussed in this book.

Listed below are some items to answer daily to help keep you motivated and on track to achieve your life's purpose.

Why?

Do you know your "why" every day? Write it down. The act of writing your goals, your "why?" every single day creates a mind-body connection that helps us articulate to ourselves what's living inside of us. It reduces worry, anxiety, and more.

"If we can write from the body, we can begin to reconnect the frayed wires between body and brain, between heart and mind, to see ourselves as whole again."
—Helene Cixous, writer and philosopher

Goals

What are the top things you are working towards for the week? It could be things all related to that new book or to learning that thing that will get you a better job. It could be tasks you need to accomplish to create that new business or a financial plan. It could be a mix of things like exercising (you committed to four times per week, so now you can track and VISUALIZE that you did it!), taking steps toward reading those homework assignments (you said you'd do it five days this week), etc. Which days did you accomplish your goals?

Visualizing your work keeps you motivated, on track, accountable. Or, if I were writing a book, the top workstreams would be writing two chapters this week, calling a publisher, meeting with the graphic designer, and sending copy to the editor.

Daily Tasks

Schedule out daily tasks in advance (take kids to school, brush teeth/shower/get dressed, etc.). You would be surprised at how much time certain tasks actually take if you are not measuring them. I do not mean use a stopwatch. Look at the clock when you walk into the bathroom and record the time. Now, remember to record exactly when you step out the door. Do this for a few days. Average the length of time, and then add ten minutes. Now you know how much to block out. If you don't block out the actual amount of time with some cushion, the rest of your day can be off schedule as a result.

Block Time

If you want to spend one part of the day to review/answer emails, block it out every day as a recurring meeting. Then, do NOT look at or respond to emails until the next email block time. Or, if you know you need to study, write that book, plan your next job move, WHATEVER it is—block it out in a two-hour or more chunk. This helps you be more productive because you are not distracted moving from one task to another. Concentration blocks = productivity!

Gratitude

Did you take time for gratitude? You will see icons on the weekly planner to remind you to take a few minutes and be grateful for someone or something. Think back in life to find something if need be.

Self-Support

Did you conduct self-support? Your air mask first! Move, eat well, sleep more, make it your intention to be happy.

Weekly/Daily Plan

Create a weekly plan to set yourself up for success for the week. Then, do your daily plan. You will be more organized on your "why" and "what" each day, ultimately moving you closer and closer to your goals.

Rather than looking at the large group of things you have to accomplish and immediately feel overwhelmed and then not take a step forward, breaking them down into manageable chunks will help you not to feel inundated and, therefore, more likely to complete. Knowing your priorities, goals, and tasks first simplifies your life because you will then block time just for those items that are important to you. This process helps weed out the clutter in your mind and allows you to focus on the priorities that matter most. Last, many of my clients find they are more relaxed and have more time. Isn't that what we all want for ourselves?

---

1. Dominican University of California, "Study focuses on strategies for achieving goals, resolutions," https://scholar.dominican.edu/cgi/viewcon tent.cgi?article=1265&context=news-releases#:~:text=Matthews%20-found%20that%20more%20than,themselves%2C%20without%20writing%20them %20down

CHAPTER 17
PLANNING

Now we know our mission and our goals and have broken them down into manageable chunks. Let's figure out how we might plan for the week ahead (many of us fall into the daily grind and do not raise our heads out of the muck to work on our personal goals we want to achieve—not just the daily grind tasks).

How do I use a planner to break things down for the week? We discussed the "how" of this effort in a previous chapter. Now, let's take a close look at what is involved in an effective method for achieving your goals.

For the week, write down your "why." Why do I need to get these things done this week? Why is this important to me? It is important to conduct this on the evening before your week begins. For most, this is a Sunday evening activity.

Next, figure out what workstreams you need to complete for the week. So, let's use the example that you are building your event-planning business. You have two clients; one needs your services for a celebration event, and the other client needs your services to plan a wedding. You have two workstreams.

Your workstream for the week could be:

Event: get pricing on three venues that have both indoor and outdoor facilities.

Wedding: get pricing on the two venues the bride chose as her top picks.

There could be many other items on your list as well. But let's stick with these for now. Next to each item, have a checkbox Monday-Sunday. After the week is underway and you have started completing these tasks, you can tick them off as complete on the weekly planning tracker.

The next section is to add anything that is extra important and the reason for the importance. For example, you need to start adding people to your team because you are getting so much more business. In this line, you would add, "Create a job posting and publish it by Friday." Now, this is a task that is important but not as tactical as the other items. In these cases, we might push that task back by another week. But if you also add the reason this is important alongside that important item to accomplish, it will help you stay on track and get it done.

For example, you might write next to that task to create a job posting, "My plan is to expand my business this year, and to remain on track, I must expand the resources needed to help me grow my business." Now when you refer back to that important item, you remind yourself of why that is so important and do not keep pushing the task out to future weeks.

I hope you can see how this system can help you stay on track. It takes a little advance planning, but it is so worth the results you will achieve when you adhere to your plan.

The next step is to write down which day you plan to conduct your top priority items for the week. You will go to your daily planner and enter that task "Create a Job Posting" as an item to accomplish at a certain time on that day. Having the mindset to plan out which day is best to do what activity means you are driving your life and not the other way around.

Daily Planner

Now, let's learn how to break your priority items down into a daily planner and to better understand the importance of the items included on each page.

The next step is to take the important items and schedule them for your day ahead. It is best practice to take the top items from your weekly planner and enter those tasks on the days you plan to work on them in advance.

Let's work on the day of activities. Open your planner to the "daily" section of the planner for that day. The first thing to do is to write your mission. It is a simple way to remember why you are showing up each day. For me, my mission was "I want to help people." In the case of the event planner and her business building, she might write, "I want to help people plan the events of their dreams."

Then, it is important to write out the big picture, the "how." How will she help people plan the events of their dreams? Her answer to that could be, "By growing my business that helps people plan the events of their dreams."

Write the goal you are working toward that day (taken from your weekly planner) to achieve that mission. Now remember, you have a lot of goals in the backlog that you will work toward, but during this week and on this day, you are working toward one or two goals, so write those down. In my case, I wanted to write a book and create a planner so I could help people identify and achieve their life's purpose. So, I would write that down next for the day.

Before answering any of the other questions, write down your entire schedule for the day. Block out things like dog-walking, taking kids to school, exercise, lunch, etc. Make sure you are blocking time for activities that are moving the needle forward for the goals that you have written about above.

Then, answer the question, "How do I want to show up today?" You might wonder why I asked that question. Let's say you need to call these venues for your event planning business today. When you stop and think about how you want to show up, you will be reminded that you are building your business. Keeping that information in mind might help you think more strategically when you speak to these venues. You might share with them about your business and that you are already bringing them potential customers. It helps you to remember to think strategically about how you will interact with the people at those venues. They can potentially return the favor and refer people to your business as well.

That example might be obvious to some but there might be little things like that which might help to move the needle even further when you stop and take the time to think about all these items as you are planning your day.

In my case, today could be:

Mission (which is my "why"): I want to help people.

How? By writing a book that will help them achieve their life's purpose.

Goals this week: call the editor to get the draft into her hands in order to meet the deadline.

How do I want to show up today? I need to make sure the editor is aware of my deadline and ensure that she can meet that goal when I speak with her. So, I need to let her know how important her work is to me (I basically rely on an editor to help me get my thoughts in order when I write) and that I am respectful of her time. I want to maintain a strong working relationship, be mindful of timelines, and ensure nothing is getting in the way of achieving them. So, I would write that down to remind myself in advance about how I want that conversation to go.

What is a successful outcome for that discussion that I wish to achieve? When people take the time to do this type of planning in advance, they are more self-aware and have better outcomes. You might even go as far as thinking, *What if she says she can't meet the deadline?* I would need to think of a plan B or remind her of our agreed-upon delivery dates or whatever might be the plan B or even plan C next step.

People who think strategically like this are more often than not successful in their endeavors. This process has helped me think more strategically, and the system helps me stay on track to achieve my goals. I know it can help you, too.

The next section to complete on your daily planner is "What am I grateful for?"

This is what you can fill out at the beginning of each day to help get you out of your busy, swirling thoughts and to instead think about your kids, the drive into work, the delicious coffee in your hand, the person who let you get ahead of them in line the other day. Whatever it is, write it down. It helps to relax your mind, get centered and focused for the day ahead, and be thankful. When we start the day with thanks for others, it helps us to be more positive and happier. Taking the time to think this through and spending a few minutes savoring the feeling helps set the tone for the day.

Reflection

Here is the last thing you do at the end of your working day. Take a few minutes, grab your journal, and think about your day. What went well? What can be improved? What did you learn today? You might even write what you are grateful for at the end of this day to close it out. When we take the time to reflect like this each day, we do not let days go by without savoring the things we actually accomplished. One of my greatest difficulties was coming up with a list of things I accomplished over the last quarter.

I was always of the mindset that unless you heard otherwise, you were on track and doing a great job. But I have learned that it is important to track your accomplishments so you remember them at the end of that quarter. This is also helpful when you need examples of what you have accomplished to bring to your boss when talking about a promotion request or salary raise.

Another reason for reflection is to measure yourself. Did you learn something new? Are you accomplishing your goals more days than not? This practice of reflection helps to measure where you are, and as you look back on previous days, you can begin to spot trends. For example, you might be really happy for a few weeks and do great things; they are tracked for your review. But then, you find that there are a few more recent weeks where you just were not that happy. You can look back on the reflections and potentially pinpoint where things were not going as expected. There was a period when I did not reflect for an entire week and was becoming very unhappy. I thought about why I was not conducting the reflection, and it was because things were really going sideways for me. When it came to reflection, I had a negative view of everything, so I did not want to even write about it. I went back and reflected on why that was and wrote down a lot of insights as to what was going on that I could have done better or handled differently.

Now when I do not feel compelled to write a daily reflection, I dig in deeper and use the 5 Whys technique to determine the root cause of the behavior. Once I know the reason and am consciously thinking about it, I can take steps to mitigate or make changes to improve my circumstances.

The daily process of writing down what you are grateful for, what you have accomplished, and learned helps you because it is self-rewarding. More importantly, it is self-acknowledging. This practice helps us grow; we begin to think twice before doing something and also reflect on our past. It is also a great way to see just how far you have progressed. There are numerous benefits to this practice. It is important to conduct it daily. Remember, it is your soul that you are investing in. You are worthwhile, and that investment will pay dividends in the long run.

Productivity Blockers

Do you ever feel resistance to sitting down to do something hard? Yeah, that's normal. When I was working toward my undergraduate degree, I noticed that I would sit down to start studying and instead would look around at how messy the apartment was. In reality, it was not messy, but I would FIND things to focus on and do instead of sitting down to study. As a result, my apartment got really clean! Ultimately, I was able to study, but I did not accomplish as much as I could have if I had been more focused.

These are techniques our minds create to avoid doing the hard stuff. Have you ever thought about what distractions you use? Maybe you want to write a book, but you never schedule it into your life. When you sit down to start it, you think to yourself, *This is too hard. I'm going to go shopping.* Maybe you go mow the lawn, surf the internet, or check social media instead. There are tons of distractions and tons of techniques we put in place to allow us to take the easy path forward. However, there are also many techniques you can put in place that will impact your productivity.

The feeling you have is resistance. Look, there is no easy path to success. So here is what works for me—make the easy things hard. In other words, lower your resistance to doing the hard things and increase resistance to the easy things. Let's start with the easy stuff and how to make it more difficult to go do the easy stuff.

If you are sitting down to write a book, for example, make it hard to get to your phone by placing your phone in another room or by turning it off and keeping it out of sight. You might even turn off wi-fi in the house so you do not allow the temptation to surf on your laptop to take hold. Do these things *before* you plan to sit down and do the task, not when you have committed to actually working on it.

Next, make the hard stuff easier to do. Clearing the clutter around your workspace and having all the things you need to work on, making certain the hard thing is close by and in easy reach so you are not tempted to get up and walk away where you might get distracted. I knew I needed to write this book, so I made an Excel spreadsheet (Excel is my life!) that listed the outline in rows. Then, in each column header across the top, I added things like "chapter name," "description," "why this chapter is needed," "citations needed," etc.

That helped make it easier for me to then focus on my book. I had some foundational writing queues when I started writing, which helped me tremendously.

You can do the same thing with working on a presentation for work. Open an Excel spreadsheet and write out all the steps you need to take for the presentation to be completed. You could make it simple and categorize it into meeting logistics—and list out all the things that need to be included, completed, practiced, etc. Then, consider who can help you with those items. List those people you need to contact and what they need to help with. Make sure they have free time available on their calendars so that they will attend. For the presentation itself, list the main points you wish to make. List out the intended audience of the presentation. Then, think about the topic, how much time it will take to present, what questions you need to answer, and by whom. After the presentation, ask yourself: *How will I follow up? What decisions are needed?* and *How will everything be implemented?*

Those are just a few ideas to help you get organized and make difficult things easier to do. This preparation accomplishes a lot, such as making it easier to break down the work into groups and see the number of tasks that you will need to accomplish for what seems like *just* a presentation.

Make certain these items are on your calendar. Block off at least two hours for your creativity to begin to flow when you are actually on that part of the work. Listing all the other tasks, knowing they are on the calendar, and grouping things on an Excel spreadsheet, mind map, or whatever tool helps you to clarify your thoughts more effectively and frees up your brain to not worry about anything else. At the same time, you get into that state of mind called flow. A flow state is when you can forget about time (set your phone to schedule time blocks—more on that in a moment). When your mind is free of the clutter, your mind will then be able to focus on what you need to get done right now and not worry or get distracted. It is a game-changer!

Okay, this leads me to the topic of balancing your calendar. I was a person who never wrote anything down because I did not set goals for myself. I allowed the river of life to sweep me along and never thought about getting onto the shore and figuring out where I wanted to go in my life. Getting clear on my purpose and my reasons for the goals (my "why") enabled me to create goals. But what happens is that things change every day. I remember having my calendar so pristine at the beginning of the week. I had blocked out time for focusing on important items and even had my work outs scheduled and lunch plans with a friend. Well, an unplanned event happened and all my pre-planning had to get shifted around or even into the following week to accommodate this unplanned event. There will be many days like this. The important thing is to leave some flexibility in your schedule for unplanned occurrences.

Then, the difficult part became finding time on my calendar. Nothing worked out because in the past there was always something that would arise every day and throw my calendar into the abyss. There are a few ways to handle these types of unplanned activities. One way is to block a two-hour window during some part of your day allocated to these types of requests. Then, also have a two-hour block scheduled that is designed for something you need to focus on and stick to your decision that you made to block time off to work on that thing. Another way to look at it would be to plan your day each morning before work starts or at the end of each day for the next day. Determine what your top three priorities are for that day (these should be based on your weekly goals which are based on quarterly, etc.).

Once you know what task you absolutely must accomplish for that day, block off and protect the time block to work on that one thing. Do it first thing in your day (as close to the first thing as you can manage) and get it checked off your list. That way, when the rest of the day comes flying in and taking up your time, you have already completed the most important items in advance.

Another technique I find helpful is the Eisenhower Matrix. In order to get a handle on your day, you need a quick decision-making method to quickly figure out what to do with all the incoming requests. President Eisenhower devised the Eisenhower Matrix to determine the importance level of each incoming request. As you move up the ladder of success, you will have more tasks to manage. The best thing you can learn as a new manager is to become super-efficient at delegating.

Most new managers are used to doing the work themselves, which is inefficient and doesn't grow their team. Instead, it helps to use the Eisenhower Matrix to categorize what to work on immediately, what items to delegate, and what can wait (meaning you do not do anything with them immediately). Eisenhower was a very busy man with a multitude of responsibilities. Eisenhower "was incredibly accomplished and was able to manage his different roles with tact, grace, and efficiency. After his terms as President, Eisenhower delivered a speech to the Second Assembly of the World Council of Churches, a fellowship of churches. In his speech, he quoted J. Roscoe Miller, the 12th president of Northwestern University, who said, 'The urgent are not important, and the important are never urgent.'"[1]

Here is how it works:

	Urgent	Less Urgent
Important	DO FIRST	SCHEDULE
Less Important	DELEGATE	DELETE

Look at an incoming task that needs to be completed. For example, let's say you get an email request to find an approval and send it to another person. Using the table above, you determine that the request is not urgent because it can wait until the next few days before it becomes a problem. In that case, you categorize it as less urgent but important. Now, what do you do with it? Let's take a deeper dive into what actions you would take based on how you prioritized above. According to the table below, you would still identify it as important but less urgent so you would schedule it.

	Urgent	Less Urgent
Important	DO FIRST	SCHEDULE
Less Important	DELEGATE	DELETE

Do first:

This should be your first area of focus for the day or should be a same-day deliverable.

Schedule:

These items are important, but you don't have to get them done immediately. Schedule time on your calendar to get these tasks done. (This should be in your two-hour window in the afternoon to work on these types of requests.)

Delegate:

Make sure to also put a system in place to follow up on the person to whom you delegated the work to ensure it is completed until you are comfortable with that person's ability to take on tasks and get things done without anyone looking over their shoulder.

Don't Do:

There are requests that might come in that are not important and far from urgent. Don't do them right now. Create a folder in your email box where you drag and drop these requests so they don't clutter your inbox.

This is an extremely effective tool, and once you start using it, you will quickly make decisions on tasks that you need to work on and leave less important tasks to others or ignore them entirely, making you more efficient and focused during your day.

There are numerous types of programs available online to research, so figure out which ones work for you. There is no one-size-fits-all solution out there. Everyone is different. The key is to start implementing goal-setting, get it on your calendar, and block off time to do it. It really is that simple.

Another important principle that you must follow is to protect your time by enforcing your calendar. Do not allow others to use your schedule to fit their needs. Rather, push out a meeting until you have time on your calendar to fit it in. Of course, there will be emergencies and high-priority items that might take precedence. Those scenarios should be few and far between.

Using these techniques with my clients, they immediately stop being overwhelmed and return to being productive.

I hope it helps you, too!

---

1. The Decision Lab, "The Eisenhower Matrix," https://thedecisionlab.com/reference-guide/management/the-eisenhower-matrix

CHAPTER 18
JUST SAY "NO."

"No" is the most simple and powerful word you have in your arsenal. Now that we know about tasks versus opportunities, how can we politely but firmly say "no" to work that leads nowhere? There are a few things to consider before I explain how.

First, women do not always say "no." Research shows that women volunteer in order to make sure the work gets done while men are more concerned about NOT doing what they consider to be trivial work. We are generally classified as the caretakers in this society. Research also shows that in households with two-income earners, with couples of opposite genders, the care of the household, children, and errands fall mainly on women. "Women are still doing the majority of housework when living with a male partner, a new study has found.

According to the analysis conducted by University College London (UCL) and published in the journal *Work, Employment and Society*, 'gender norms remain strong' when it comes to household chores.

They discovered that women do approximately 16 hours of

household chores every week, while men do closer to six. Many women refer to this as "the second shift."

Furthermore, women did the bulk of the domestic duties in 93 percent of the couples analysed for the study."[1]

As Dr. Vanessa Bohns, Ph.D. and professor of organizational behavior at Cornell University, said for the *Wall Street Journal:* "One of our most fundamental needs is for social connection and a feeling that we belong. Saying 'no' feels threatening to our relationships and that feeling of connectedness."

Unsurprisingly, women are more likely to say "yes" even if they want to say "no." In the words of academic coach Mary McKinney, Ph.D., for the American Psychological Association, "Saying no is more challenging for women because of societal pressures to be likable. Men are still seen as likable if they're assertive, while women are more likely to be seen as likable if they're compliant." Unfortunately, the pressure to be likable is even bigger for minority women.

Second, if you are a person who is passionate about her job, you are more likely to take on more work but also more likely to be taken advantage of. According to an article printed in the *Journal of Personality and Social Psychology* entitled "Understanding contemporary forms of exploitation: Attributions of passion serve to legitimize the poor treatment of workers," the researchers found that people consider it more legitimate to make passionate workers do more tasks like working weekends (unpaid) and handling issues that were not in the job description.

This understanding is important but makes it more difficult when your boss asks you to take on more work, especially if you are new in the workforce or to a company and you are trying to establish your personal brand. In the long run, it is unhealthy for you and the company. Respecting your boundaries creates more respect for yourself. The more respect you have for yourself, the less overwhelm you have in your life because you respect your work/life balance and take steps to ensure it is reinforced.

I have seen co-workers work grueling hours claiming a passion for their work. Eventually, it leads to burnout, exhaustion, and finally, to feeling discouraged and disillusioned.

Getting back to equality at home, it is important to ensure all chores are distributed equitably. One way to do that is to estimate the amount of time spent on each activity. Then, propose a possible equitable distribution scenario and meet with your partner to review and discuss who will do what.

This might sound excessive to some readers. However, consider things like managing your finances. In order to get a handle on getting your finances in order, you must look at your spending versus income. To truly understand and make changes in your spending, you must know exactly where your money is going. To do that, you have to list every single line item of spending, from drinks with friends to parking fees to that cup of coffee on the way into work. If you do not know where your money is spent, you cannot know how to reduce spending. The same concept applies to chores. You both live in the same place, so chores to maintain the household should be equitably split as well. The point of this exercise is not to be completely exact, but to realize where you are spending your time, how it can be more equitably distributed, what can be delegated, and how you can structure your day so that these tasks are on the calendar and accounted for.

Once you have all of this information, now you know why you are saying "no." The conversation is a lot more effective when you outline it on paper and make the work visual. Otherwise, the conversation is more esoteric and not based on facts.

That approach helps to build the case for yourself. It is reasonable, and it is doable. Now, the problem becomes your fear of not speaking up for yourself and not having the conversation or writing this step off as silly or meaningless. It is not. Pay attention to what doubts arise as you think about doing this exercise. Then, refer to Chapter 23 on fear to learn how to address your self-doubt. You will start to be the change you want to see when you follow this process.

Now, how do you apply this concept at work?

Look at all the meetings on your calendar over the past several months. Write down some themes about what they relate to and why they are important. List them out on a spreadsheet (or paper, or whatever format works for you) and start to categorize them as "task," "opportunity," and "strategy."

Next, start tracking the actual work you are performing on a daily/weekly/monthly basis that was not on your calendar (hint: put all work on your calendar, make a thirty-minute block to respond to emails, another block to work on other people's tasks, requests, etc.). Over a day or two, you will have a solid understanding of where you are spending your time.

After you have categorized the work, figure out what percentage of time you are working on tasks versus opportunities, versus tasks that are strategic in nature (thinking about a big project that you want to implement and taking time to ideate, focusing on your career top three goals, etc.). Look at the percentage of time you spend on tasks that can be delegated (yes, it takes more time up-front to delegate but that is only in the initial stages) to junior team members, to volunteers, etc. Have you actually said "no" to any work yet? Cleaning up the clutter so you can focus on opportunities and strategies will move you forward to reach your goals more efficiently and effectively.

Once you have mastered this step, when new work comes your way and you use the Eisenhower Matrix to categorize its importance, you will have a clearer understanding of the priority, which will lead you to decide to do the task, delegate it, or set it aside.

The next phase is to look at incoming work that is more task-oriented or considered as low-value projects that you can truly say no because you are clear on exactly the work (and types of work) you have in front of you.

You will think in terms of bartering with your boss. For example, you might say, "Yes, I will take this on because I have this window of opportunity for the next four weeks, but in return, I want (insert coveted project here) so I can build my skills and achieve my career goals."

Half the battle of saying "no" occurs because we don't believe we are doing much work. We are sure that we can take on something else. In reality, you have a ton of tasks that are taking up too much of your time—so much so that you cannot focus on the items that help your career move forward, like strategy and opportunities. Therefore, when your boss does ask, you can honestly say "no" and simply list out the facts. For example, you might say, "That luncheon is not something I have bandwidth to put together because I have 3 strategic vendor contracts under negotiation, 6 dashboards to compile for our next board meeting, and 4 client presentations due by the end of the month which will require 100% of my focus."

Now, how to say "no" and mean it! This is an entire course all on its own!

Agreeing to work on too many assignments and raising your hand to help in too many projects will leave you stretched thin, overwhelmed, and stressed. Learning the art of saying "no" is crucial to your success and the success of the company. You protect your boundaries and deliver better quality work. When employees take on too much, they become overwhelmed and burned out. You can reach a point where you get sick as a result. Burnout is real.

While there might be some truth to the belief that there just is no good way to deliver bad news, here are some ways in which to make saying "no" to someone go as well as it can.

Always remain calm when giving bad news, state supporting facts associated with reasons why, and then summarize by saying (think of *Shark Tank*), "And for those reasons, I'm out!" Seriously, you are not a quitter and would not make that statement. But having a calm demeanor with logical reasons to support your position will go a long way to ensure you will deliver the bad news in the best way possible.

Next, practice saying "no." Starting at home helps prepare you for work requests. When you list out all the other items for which you are responsible and have a true grasp on timing, it lets your boss know that you are in touch with the amount of your work and that you each item seriously. Your boss will also understand that, in order to deliver effectively, you cannot take on any more assignments until ____ (name a date or leave it blank); you can just end your statement there. If you want to throw a lifeline, tell your boss when you'd have more free time to take on this additional work. It is always best to be viewed as reasonable, a team player and not be viewed as a "no" person.

Here are some other tips:

Clearly assessing the task request using your existing priorities list and the Eisenhower Matrix, then determining if this request will create career opportunities for you will go a long way towards being reasonable if you plan to decline a task. In addition, ask yourself, "Will this request enable me to assemble a team of people to lead?" If so, this is another possible way to increase your skills and showcase your performance as a leader.

Also, determine any repercussions of saying "no." We always think there will be repercussions, but be honest and realistic in your assessment.

It also is important to be honest and straightforward with your response. One of the things we do as women is self-deprecate instead of standing in our power and being straightforward. I love Amy Cuddy's approach, which is to take a power pose. For more information, watch her Ted Talk "Body Language May Shape Who

You Are." The moment you do that power pose that she recommends, the more you feel powerful. If you have taken into account all the work you are currently doing and you have absolutely no bandwidth to take the work on but are afraid to stand up for yourself, practicing the power stance might be the thing you need to start incorporating to feel grounded in your body and mind. This practice is not a cure-all or a solution to insecurity but rather one technique of many that might help you have more confidence when you need it.

Have trade-offs in your back pocket, too. You can always explain the workload you currently have and say to your boss, "I would not be able to deliver the quality work you know I deliver should I overextend by taking on this project." You can also offer to help on a portion of the project that you know you can do easily. That way, you are extending a lifeline of sorts.

Another thing to note is the double-bind women find themselves in. There are many examples, but the one that best describes this scenario is that men expect women to take on tasks, not to say "no," and to just do what needs to be done. When women speak up and decline to take on more work, we can be deemed as a non-team player or someone who always says "no." But don't jump to that conclusion right away and simply take the work. Instead, apply the options described thus far. Then, make your decision. Be neutral in your body language and voice, make your case, and if there is no way out, then there's nothing you can do other than to get other team members to help and shoulder some of the responsibility where possible.

Bottom line: there are times when you cannot say "no" to additional work. However, it is important to create boundaries and stand firm in a neutral but strong manner. In addition, don't leave work early or take too many or extra-long breaks if you really do have a heavy workload. Think about the optics.

Last, don't sweat the small stuff. If you are a people-pleaser, you might take on the work anyway because you don't want the other person to be mad at you. The only thing I have to say to that is personal accountability. You can and should only be accountable for your work. If your boss or co-worker asks you to do more, then look at your current workload. Is this new request something you can truly take on given your current work deliverables? Make sure you are not taking it on to be nice. You are accountable for your behavior, not anyone else's. If someone does not like that you cannot take on more work because you have a full workload already, the problem belongs to the person trying to give you more work. They will have to figure out a solution. In this situation, it would mean that you have made a reasonable case for why you cannot take on the additional work at this time. You've stated your case factually, calmly, and maybe even offered an alternative solution. After that, this request and the associated work does not belong to you. Think of whatever task as a hot potato. People just want to get rid of it as fast as possible. But you do not have to take the potato. Just don't play the game! You need to learn not to take things personally, and don't assume someone will be upset because you said "no."

The more you practice, the better you become. Listening to yourself as you practice is helpful. Even recording yourself in a recording app where you can see your facial expressions and hear your tone of voice, like on Microsoft Teams or Zoom, is worth doing if you have trouble standing up for yourself.

When you enforce boundaries, it shows others that you respect your time and that you are being intentional about what you are spending your time on. It is not personal, and you are not a bad person for saying "no." In fact, it's the opposite. You know exactly what you can do, what is on your plate, and are thinking clearly about delivering high-quality/high-value work. In order to do that effectively, you cannot agree to do everything.

When you say "no," it is not easy, but it is essential. As in your private life, in your work, you must state and enforce your boundaries in such a way as to not over-apologize, get your message across firmly, politely, and respectfully. In this way, you learn to stop putting others' needs ahead of your own.

While it may not be easy at first, it is a skill worth developing.

---

1. Independent UK, "Women still do majority of household chores, study finds," https://www.independent.co.uk/life-style/women-men-household-chores-domestic-house-gender-norms-a9021586.html

CHAPTER 19
SELF-ADVOCACY

Women fear self-advocacy due to our societal and cultural norms. Let's be honest here. Think about a time when you were a kid, and you just finished a paper or won a kickball game or did something about which you were so proud. You would go tell everybody about your accomplishment—your parents, your friends, your teacher, and anyone who would listen. But over time, your teachers start to say, "don't brag," because you are a girl and then your friends made fun of you because they labeled you as a "bragger."

From a young age, and then reinforced in school, women learn not to speak up, that we are not as important as men. This belief impacts everything we do in later life and explains one of the reasons women are not great at self-advocacy. There are numerous studies to support the fact that women are less likely than men to self-advocate. Please read "Women's Bragging Rights: Overcoming Modesty Norms to Facilitate Women's Self-Promotion" for more information. [1]

There is a book I would recommend you read in order to learn self-advocacy that focuses on learning how to conduct self-promotion without sounding as though you are bragging about your accomplishments. That book is Peggy Klaus' *Brag! The Art of Tooting Your Own Horn Without Blowing It* (Warner, 2003). The purpose of this effort is to have the ability to sell yourself in such a way as to not come across in a negative manner.

Another great piece of advice is to find a sponsor. In this case, a sponsor is someone who might recommend you for a role. They might also get you into that meeting where decisions are being made so you can learn more and be exposed to other leaders. In other words, a mentor is typically a more senior leader invested in your career success. The problem with that is finding a sponsor! There is yet another book that might help you as you work toward that goal called *(Forget a Mentor) Find a Sponsor* by Silvia Ann Hewlett.

Many women do well in school because, when they put in the work, they generally get rewarded based on what they produced in terms of grades. As a result, women learn to work hard and believe that if they put in the work that they will get recognized. The problem with this approach is that this method doesn't work in the corporate world. Here are the main societal beliefs that dominate Western society:

- Women are expected to be modest and not self-advocate; men are expected to self-advocate.
- Men are expected to be assertive, dominant, and bold, while women are expected to be selfless, caring, and submissive. Therefore, women who do self-advocate are less likely to be liked, and their self-advocacy will be seen as excessive compared with the same self-advocacy by men.
- Women are great at advocating for others and are expected to do so.

- Women feel uncomfortable, uninterested, and unmotivated in tasks that require self-advocacy and don't perform as well as a result.

Many of the women who come to me for coaching struggle with advocacy and speaking up for themselves. In one case, a woman named Linda came to me and shared that she was consistently seeing others get promoted. But those women were not working as hard as Linda, did not have as many projects on their plates as she did, and were not putting in the number of hours Linda was.

The issue was that Linda was not speaking up for herself and not conducting self-advocacy for her own benefit. Yet others were, and they were the ones getting ahead and attaining coveted promotions.

After working with Linda, I helped her realize that she needed to reassess her strategy, incorporate the practices shared here, like tracking her wins, share soundbites with her boss, and create lunch-and-learns to showcase across divisions the work she was accomplishing and based on the value she brings and has already brought to the company. I am proud to say this client achieved a 30% salary increase. Salary increases can happen for you, too, when you implement the practice of self-advocacy.

After a few months, Linda told me that she was invited to apply for another role in her company as a result of implementing these self-advocacy techniques.

Self-advocacy doesn't come across as bragging or boasting when done correctly. The results speak for themselves when you do implement this in your daily practice.

Missing Out on Opportunities

Not only do we NOT do a great job at advocating for ourselves in our current roles, but we lose career opportunities. These losses happen when we don't go after roles for which we have the right skills and enough experience because we doubt ourselves and never apply.

How does that impact women financially? It can mean half a million dollars over the lifetime of your career. For example, if you are making $82,000 per year, there is likely a man who does a similar job to you, earning $100,000 per year doing the same type of work.

To bring home the significance of that pay disparity, let's break down what that looks like over the course of your entire career. By the time you are ready for retirement, you, as a woman, will have earned $540,000 less than your average male counterpart if you are 30 years old at the start of this scenario and remained at that salary for 30 years until you retired at 60. The male counterpart is the same age and his salary never changes either.

That means you could have had over a half-million dollars more to add to your retirement. You might have been able to purchase a house in a better school district so your children had a better education. The worst part is that you and your male counterpart would both get pay raises, but you would never catch up. In fact, the current trajectory would indicate that the total amount of $540,000 would widen even further. These numbers are, generally speaking, even worse if you are a woman of color.

Let's look at the same scenario, but we'll say that each of you receives a 3% increase in salary each year for those same 30 years. The difference between being a woman in that scenario is that you will earn $882,000 less than your male counterpart. That is a huge disparity throughout your career.

I hope this clarifies why you need to learn to advocate for yourself. The earlier you start, the better your income potential throughout your career. You need to advocate for yourself in your current role, when applying for a new role, and when negotiating your salary.

Another client I worked with came to me after she implemented self-advocacy and, as a result, was offered a promotion. She was grappling with the idea of the company offering a promotion without a salary increase.

This can happen for you too when you implement the practice of self-advocacy.

How to Self-Advocate

It appears that it should be easy to speak up for yourself. The truth is that society still has us in a double bind. Research indicates there are costs associated with resisting gender stereotypes. First, when a woman speaks up and states a fact about her work, that behavior is perceived as being exaggerated. If a man does the same thing, he is viewed as being assertive. In this case, women are viewed as being out of the role they are supposed to play (meaning they should be meek, submissive, etc.).

There are also social costs associated with women speaking up. Simply because she is a woman, her statement is viewed as too "self-promoting," and she is less liked by her peers. A woman who self-promotes is viewed generally as being a higher performer but not as well-liked because of the perceived exaggerated view of her performance.

From an advancement perspective, leaders are chosen partially for their likeability. Being seen as "too self-promoting" may hinder your chances for promotion.

So, as a woman, what are your options? In a culture that insists on self-advocacy and discounts you when you do self-advocate, it appears that there is no way to win.

The best advice is to understand your professional strengths. List your accomplishments and keep track of them so that when you go for your annual review or seek a new role, you have them at your fingertips when needed. It is also important to communicate your professional strengths to your peers, mentors, managers, and even future employers.

Most women will, over time, build trust, strengthen relationships, and focus on their reputation as someone who gets things done, gets results, and follows through. Only then do they feel as though they can advocate for themselves or feel confident in the value they bring to the organization. But that does take time. It is worth doing, however; tracking your accomplishments will help you keep things fresh in your mind.

As humans, we tend to remember the bad things that happen. Our brains are wired to do so. Therefore, writing down your accomplishments will help build your confidence while remembering all the contributions and value you bring to the table. Next, I suggest practicing writing your accomplishments in the form of PAS. P= the problem, A = the actions you took, and then S = the solution. This should be a quick and short statement. It works best when you add in metrics to showcase savings or efficiencies. Here is a quick example:

PROBLEM: One of my most recent projects was behind schedule when I was assigned to lead the work.

ACTIONS: I quickly assessed the work left to accomplish, built relationships with the new team I was tasked with leading, and determined the critical path and where we could shorten timelines.

SOLUTION: The outcome was that the project not only got back on track, but we delivered two weeks early, created a savings of [$X], and improved team performance.

Here are more tips for how to advocate for yourself:

1. Speak up and ask for what you want. We as women rarely take the time to sit down and think about what we want, but it is important to take note of what you want in your career and to ask for it.

2. Show pride in your work; don't downplay your accomplishments. If you notice yourself giving credit to other people or the team when you are complimented (this is called deflecting), rein that in and learn to simply say, "Thank you."

3. Document your wins and the ways you have made contributions to the organization. By keeping a running list of your wins and contributions in the workplace, as mentioned earlier, you have several examples fresh in your mind and documented for sharing as needed when gearing up for performance reviews, year-end bonus considerations, or when you are interviewing. What are you doing really well? How have you furthered your organization's mission? In what ways do you go above and beyond in your role? During your quarterly or annual reviews, come prepared to point to your accomplishments in a matter-of-fact way. If you want to ask for a raise, you can use this list as a way to demonstrate your value and get paid accordingly.

4. Add visibility to your work through lunch-and-learns, workshops, or use other means to showcase your work and gain exposure to other areas of the company. Create physical, transparent records of your work, such as status reports you can share across teams. You might consider sharing these status reports with other leaders outside your area who might benefit from learning about the work you are doing.

If you are not getting the credit you deserve, don't hesitate to move to another position or company where you're valued for your contributions.

5. Advocate for yourself when you are in salary negotiations. Unfortunately, women are more likely than men to accept an initial job offer without first negotiating their salary. Over the years when you do not negotiate for more salary, your salary will continue to trend downward over the course of your employment. According to a study conducted by Randstad,[2] almost 60% of women have never negotiated their pay with an employer. Asking for more money can be a challenging prospect for women who are conditioned to not speak up. It is important to research and know your worth. That is where the importance comes from tracking your list of wins and contributions. Also, realize that your male counterparts are likely already tracking their wins and negotiating a higher salary for themselves. The first salary offer is expected to be an opening bid upon which you should make your counteroffer. That potential employer expects that you will negotiate. When women realize and fully embrace their worth, things change. One example of realizing your worth is standing up for yourself in salary negotiations. This is how things change. Now is the time.

6. Make sure your work is more opportunity-focused versus task-driven. Do a review of your work. As mentioned in an earlier chapter, women frequently take on more of the tasks in the office, such as planning social events, arranging meetings, and mundane operational work versus strategic work. You might actually enjoy doing some of this type of work, and my advice is to look at how many tasks you are working on versus opportunities. I like Pareto's Principle—keep the ratio 80-20. You should aim for 80% strategic work (direct impact to the organization) and 20% focused

on tasks. If taking on these new tasks keeps you within that 80-20 ratio, go for it!

7. To prevent overwhelm, ask yourself: Are you taking on more than you can handle? Also, look around your environment to determine if the men in your department are also assigned these task-related activities. If not, feel free to decline. You can refer to your workload as an indication your plate is full, negotiate with your manager that if you take on this task-related activity, ask the manager to agree that the next strategic project goes to you in return. Last, if you are in a leadership position, assign some of the tasks to the men on your team. Even if you are an individual contributor, you can assign tasks to junior team members. If you manage project work, you are in a position to assign project-related tasks to your team, too. The goal here is to be strategic in what you will work on and what you can delegate or decline.

8. Find mentors. I have learned from my time in sales that people are afraid or do not even think to ask someone to be their mentor. But one of the other greatest learnings for me is that when you ask, most people say "yes!" People want to help others, but finding people who want mentorship is difficult. The solution is to simply ask.

The upcoming chapter will go into these insights more deeply, but the point remains that mentorship and sponsorship are both crucial to the advancement of women in the workplace.

As a career coach, I get asked almost daily about whether or not women should go back to school, get that certification, etc. My advice is to always continue your education because it stretches you as a human, and when we stretch ourselves mentally, we grow. Growth is key to success in life. However, because we never feel good enough and/or we believe that we need all these credentials to prove our worth, we sometimes find ourselves going after that degree for the wrong reasons. Ask yourself if this degree/certification/diploma is essential to you getting into that next role. Before you say "yes," really do your research and look at men in the roles you want to be in, what degrees/certifications do they possess?

There will be obvious degrees like medical and law degrees, but there are others like MBA's that are more opaque in terms of value to your career. I could write an entire book on getting master's degrees and when they are important and when they are not. Bottom line: I want you to consistently learn and achieve. But I also want you to do it for the right reasons. An MBA doesn't immediately translate into a managerial role. You might consider volunteer work where you can gain experience leading work and/or people. That real-life experience will help you get the leadership skills needed to move up. So, if you want to advance, consider all the options you have available to gain those skills for your continued growth. Look at leaders inside and outside of your organization to determine their areas of responsibility, where they worked, what jobs they held, their education/certifications, etc. By taking the time to research this information, you will be in a better position to answer the "education or not" question for yourself. If most leaders have an advanced degree, for example, then follow their example if that is the role that you seek. Last, let your manager know you are building these skills, gaining experience, or getting the degree/certification to contribute even more value to the organization.

9. If you can see it, you can be it! Make sure to be a role model for how to be the best self-advocate you can be. By modeling this behavior, it helps show future generations of women how to advocate for themselves. Be that mentor to the next generation of women. When you show women how to get respect and ask for

and expect to be paid their worth, you are teaching countless others that women can ask for and expect equal treatment. Let's make sure this way of being becomes non-negotiable in our society. As mentioned earlier, when women know their worth, the world positively changes.

Build Your Team of Trusted Advisors

When she came to me, my client, Angelica, was the lone wolf. We worked together to help Angelica tap into a network of trusted advisors that she created. As a result, Angelica was pushing the envelope on her comfort levels and learning to do things she had not done before because she had the support of the network she had built. This support system enabled Angelica to practice difficult conversations—like speaking up for herself, sharing her contributions, and even learning new ideas on how to conduct self-advocacy.

Angelica shared, "After years of going it alone, I now practice with my network. I even find it motivating. I can get past my fears with the support of an amazing network of work friends and colleagues. If I ever feel the fear of advocating for myself creeping back in, then I have a great support system that I can bounce ideas off of and practice with before I go in front of my boss or others."

The journey does not need to be traveled alone. You can also engage your manager to help you get more exposure to other leaders in your organization or to brainstorm with you on ideas to get your work noticed by other departments. If you have a manager who is not willing to help you, find another leader inside your organization who will. There are many leaders who wish to help, and many times, all you have to do is ask.

Sometimes, we need our trusted advisors to give us feedback on our approach. If you do not get results on your own, ask others for help. They may have ideas you had not considered. You may need to think about how you are communicating—are the folks to whom you are reaching out too busy to reply? How can you break down your message into a smaller soundbite that is tailored to that person?

Look for Ways to Create Opportunities for Yourself

There are many different ways to ensure you are not being overlooked any longer. First, assess where you are in your career and where you want to go, and then reflect on what you have done to date that supports your vision. What is your personal brand? What things can you do in order to get more exposure across teams or departments? Do you have your list of wins readily available to pitch to someone you might meet in the hallway or during a meeting? When you are clear, you have a better chance of snagging those opportunities.

If you have been reaching out to another department leader without success, have you researched what they are trying to solve? How can the work you have accomplished to date help you share your accomplishments in such a way as to indicate you can be part of the solution?

Here is an example of where self-advocacy helped me in my career. I was working as a sales leader in a technology firm where I saw that new sales folks were not implementing the mandatory sales training the company had spent a large sum of money on to improve sales. I was new to the firm and was looking for an opportunity to establish myself. I noticed this with my sales team and asked other sales leaders if they had witnessed the same phenomenon. It turns out that they were. I pitched the idea of creating a sales coaching and certification program for the entire sales team to senior leadership, who agreed this would be a program they would love to sponsor. The net result of this program was that sales folks were going to market with consistent marketing messaging, booking truly qualified leads in the pipeline, and increased sales. By reaching out with a solution to a problem I identified, I helped solidify my brand in the company and furthered my career considerably.

To summarize, here are some final thoughts:

1. Create your trusted advisor network.
2. Ask for others to advocate on your behalf.
3. Remember that your fear of speaking up is not holding only you back but countless other women. Face your fears and break the pattern of the self-advocacy double bind. You matter, and so do all the other women you are role-modeling for.
4. Ask your trusted peers to help you practice self-advocacy, offer suggestions for improvement, and share what they see in you. You are helping them just as much as you are helping yourself.
5. Prepare! Have that list of wins in your back pocket at all times. Rehearse saying it out loud so that it comes easily. Remember to keep it short and follow the PAS model. Click here to get a document to help familiarize yourself with the model: www.kennedyeffect.com/downloads.

---

1. Sage Journals, "Women's Bragging Rights: Overcoming Modesty Norms to Facilitate Women's Self-Promotion," https://journals.sagepub.com/doi/10.1177/0361684313515840?icid=int.sj-abstract.similar-articles.1
2. Ranstad USA, "Salary insights and trends," https://rlc.randstadusa.com/for-business/learning-center/future-workplace-trends/randstad-2020-compensation-insights?utm_campaign=rusa_Salary+Guide+2020_client_rus_all&utm_medium=press&utm_source=prnewswire,

CHAPTER 20
HOW TO LEVERAGE SUCCESS

In order to achieve success, you need help. Sure, you can go it alone, but it will take longer than if you leveraged support from others. Rapid and sustained growth is done most effectively when working with a coach who has experience in the areas in which you need help and knows how to help you learn quickly and move forward.

There are so many incredible benefits of working with a coach. According to the Institute of Coaching, a not-for-profit organization,[1]

> "...80% of people who receive coaching report increased self-confidence, and over 70% benefit from improved work performance, relationships, and more effective communication skills...coaching provides an invaluable space for personal development."

A coach will help you make a positive impact on your career. There are so many areas where you can choose to work with a coach that will make a difference in your ability to achieve results more quickly than working alone. In fact, research has shown that coaching creates an effective impact in organizations as well. Further, business leaders rely on coaches to help them navigate their careers. Most people do not think about the notion of hiring a coach. However, when you consider the evidence that coaching does help people improve, it's surprising that more people don't seek out a coach!

Let's first take a look at the definition of coaching. ICF, The International Coaching Federation, defines coaching as "…partnering with clients in a thought-provoking and creative process that inspires them to maximize their personal and professional potential. The process of coaching often unlocks previously untapped sources of imagination, productivity, and leadership."

Coaching means you must be accountable for yourself. Therefore, when something needs to change in your life, it is up to you to make that change. When working with a coach, you are the one who does the work, and the coach guides you on that journey. Many people would prefer to just get the information instead of making a change in their lives.

People often believe that to use a coach effectively, you need to know what you want. Most people do not know what they want, so they cannot envision how to use a coach to help them. The truth is that a good coach can help them figure this out. Coaches can work with a client to help them get crystal clear on what they want for their lives or career—or both.

People sometimes would rather speak with a therapist to talk through things than hire a coach. There are important reasons to seek therapy, and I am a huge believer in the practice of therapy. But when a person is seeking ways in which to improve their career, achieve success, develop capabilities, or even which capabilities upon which to focus, a coach is the right choice. In working with hundreds of women, I have noticed that we have learned to go it alone and are reluctant to go to those uncomfortable moments necessary to truly grow.

We might also feel embarrassed that we are weak in some ways and feel like we should already know what to do in order to attain success in our careers and in life. In fact, many women go inward and blame their unhappiness on themselves. We tend to think we should just be happy with the way things are.

Maria came to me when she was struggling with a decision she knew she needed to make about her job. Maria had been in the company for over ten years. Initially, she moved into new roles quickly and received a salary to match. However, for the previous four years, she felt as though her career was stagnant and did not understand how to move ahead. All the tactics Maria had used in the past were no longer working to move her forward. Yet Maria kept working hard, putting in long hours, hoping her boss would notice.

After working with me for just under a few months, Maria completely transformed. She could see her own roadblocks and learned to move them out of the way. Maria began advocating for herself. She also incorporated other techniques specific to her situation that I helped coach her through and landed herself a new job at another firm with a 25% salary increase. Maria said, "I wish I had come to you earlier! I spent four years trying to make this type of transition happen, and you helped me in just a few short months."

Later, Maria confided in me and said I helped her have better relationships with her new working peers and helped her quickly get up-to-speed in her new role—in a brand-new way. She was already making great career strides in her new company.

What about mentorship? Many of the folks with whom I work ask me about mentorship versus coaching. Mentorship is generally company-specific or career-specific. Here is one way to look at it: use a mentor to help you navigate moving up the ladder within a company itself. They recommend others to meet with, how to handle specific situations, and offer advice on which degree or degrees you should attain for success in your chosen area of interest. Mentors generally share their knowledge and skills to help a mentee grow.

How is a coach different than a mentor? A coach helps you figure out what it is you want and then suggests how to leverage a mentor inside that company to help you move forward.

After working with so many women, it has become clear to me that they need to figure out what it is they want to do before they can engage with a mentor. Most women haven't taken the time to do the work or the soul-searching to determine what they want for their lives. Most people do not invest in themselves to figure this out. As a result, many women do not even know what to say to a mentor or how to use one to help them further their careers. If they do meet with a mentor, it is very superficial and offers few incremental improvements.

Coaching is more goal-oriented and time-boxed. Mentorship can be that as well, but generally speaking, a mentor will not work with you to overcome a personal weakness you might have. You likely do not want to share that sort of thing with a mentor, given the working relationship you may have with them. Coaches have seen it all! Well, good coaches have, and they know how to direct you and help you work on the things that are blocking you from achieving success. Further, a coach will help you get to the point where you will know exactly how you can leverage a mentor.

Have you heard of the quote, "Give a man a fish and you feed him for a day. Teach him how to fish and you feed him for a lifetime" from the Chinese philosopher Lao Tzu, founder of Taoism?

Coaching is more like teaching a person to fish versus handing them fish. It is also performance-based instead of career-specific.

Olivet Nazarene University surveyed 3,000 people about professional mentor-mentee relationships in 2019.

Here's what they found:

76% of people think mentors are important, however, only 37% of people currently have one.[2]

Why? There are two main reasons I have found from my experience.

1. Most people do not know what they want and therefore do not know how to work with a mentor.
2. Because most people are afraid to ask!

People *want* to help other people. However, it can be daunting to walk up to someone and ask them to be your mentor. In that same study by Olivet Nazarene University, they found that only 14% of people asked someone to be their mentor.

Do not assume people are not willing to help. While working on my master's, I once asked the late Ray Anderson, the founder, and CEO of Interface, Inc., for an interview. He was famously known for being one of the first CEOs to not only discuss sustainability but was an early champion of environmental entrepreneurism. His company produced modular carpeting (carpet pieces that are in sections or squares), so instead of replacing an entire room, you could change out only the worn or damaged areas. I was granted a 1-hour interview and learned so much after speaking with such an amazing, innovative, forward-thinking, and gracious leader.

Simply asking can make all the difference in the world.

---

1. Institute of Coaching, McLean, Affiliate of Harvard Medical School, "The Personal Benefits of Coaching," https://instituteofcoaching.org/coaching-overview/coaching-benefits#:~:text=The%20benefits%20of%20coaching%20are,and%20more%20effective%20communication%20skills.&text=Coaching%20provides%20an%20invaluable%20space%20for%20personal%
2. Olivet Nazarene University, "Study explores professional mentor-mentee relationships in 2019," https://online.olivet.edu/research-statistics-on-professional-mentors

CHAPTER 21
SELF-SUPPORT

Along the way, how do you take care of yourself? Why is it important?

Taking care of yourself means that you take regular breaks during the day to stand up, walk around, or take a moment to clear your thoughts. It also means taking a time-out if you just came out of a stressful meeting. It is important because we women forget to care for ourselves, especially when we have children because we are so busy taking care of everyone else. We must take care of ourselves, so we have the ability to give back, think more clearly, reduce stress, and many other important benefits that arise when you practice taking care of yourself. Self-care is where you get up and move your body to either stretch, take a quick mindfulness session for five minutes, or relax and do a twenty-minute meditation.

The choice is yours, but the important thing is that you build it into your daily practice. Start small, but just take that first step. Next thing you know, you'll be doing it three times a day or more and feeling much calmer and more centered.

Be intentional. You don't do what you don't plan. Make your

list of your favorite things that work for you so you don't have to go figure out each day what to book in your planner. Give yourself this gift. Your body, mind, and soul will thank you!

BODY:

- Walking/running
- Yoga
- Stretching
- Cardio
- Strength training
- Warm bath

MIND:

- Be grateful
- Be happy
- Joyful—Bring joy to the room by feeling excited to be alive; others will pick up on it and feel it too
- Practice patience
- Practice kindness toward co-workers, like sharing a compliment

SOUL:

- Meditation
- Prayer
- Journaling time
- Walking in nature
- Volunteer
- Forgive someone.

Self-support is being mindful of your needs so you can be at your best every day and meet the needs of others. Taking care of yourself teaches you about yourself more deeply. When you become diligent about working out, sleeping, and eating well, you start to learn that you are good at discipline and making good choices that serve your overall well-being.

Self-support includes the items listed above but can also mean not letting someone else's actions or opinions define you. It can mean that when you make a mistake, you are more forgiving toward yourself. I know I have a voice inside my head that is actually quite mean and calls me names when I make a mistake in some circumstances. We all seem to have these negative thoughts that arise when we do something that we are not particularly proud of. The important thing is to notice the thoughts and disagree with them. Certainly, it is important to acknowledge that you might not have reacted in the best way and take a minute to acknowledge it and think of something you will do next time so that this will not happen again. Those types of actions are also self-care.

In our crazy world, we can get caught up in the belief that we have to work endless hours, not take any days off for self-care, or work even harder to ensure that we do not lose our job…and the list goes on. Even if our work demands are high, we can learn to take time out to work on ourselves, relax, take that walk, or any of the many suggestions listed in this book.

In her paper "Self-Care Through Self-Compassion: A Balm for Burnout," Susan C. Coaston writes: "Higher levels of self-compassion can serve as a buffer against burnout (Barnard & Curry, 2011). Therefore, cultivating an attitude of self-compassion may assist counselors in employing self-care practices to refresh, rejuvenate, and recharge their bodies, minds, and souls."[1]

Here, Ms. Coaston is referring to compassion that counselors need to remember to employ, but this goes for all of us working folks who work ourselves too many hours without taking time for breaks.

This is a reminder that we all need self-support. If we become burned out, we are of no use to ourselves—or anyone else for that matter. This system of practice I am writing about in this book will help you to implement self-care as part of your daily routine. It is important to remember that self-support is not just getting enough sleep a couple of nights a week; it's a complete system where you ensure mental rest throughout the day as well. Our brains require a lot of power to keep working properly. According to BrainFacts.org, our brains take up 20% of the resting state energy of the body. How many people even think about the implications? That means an average-weight person uses about 320 calories just to think!

We need to remember to rest our brains, and journaling and meditation are tools that can be used to give our brains a break. Think about how much we work out our muscles. If you are into body-building, you know that you work out one muscle group on one day and another muscle group the next, which provides the first muscle group a rest day. We need to give our brains a rest day every now and again. If we are not sleeping well or do not get up to get a change of scenery throughout the day, we are not giving our brains and bodies the rest they need to be at our best.

Remember, we cannot be successful if we do not first put on our own oxygen masks.

Meditation

Why is this important? There are many articles published online that tout the many benefits of meditation. First, let me say that I personally find great benefits from meditation. I believe it helps to calm my racing thoughts, helps me to get and feel centered at the start of my day, and helps me wind down and get ready for sleep in the evening.

All of that sounds great, right? But is it very difficult to do. In order to live a fulfilled life, you absolutely must be present to notice it. Sure, you have all heard about being present in life in order to enjoy it. But how many of us do something to make certain we are present?

Have you ever been driving into work and suddenly noticed the trees have all dropped their leaves? You drove this route every day and realized that you never even saw them change color. Or have you ever come home from work and the kids are trying to tell you all about your day but you can't focus on them because you are thinking about all the things you need to do this evening: cook meals, prep lunches, get the kids' homework done, their clothes laid out for the next day, bath time, and then you have work you need to finish up before the day is over? Then, you find yourself saying "yes" to your kids, trying to pretend like you are listening to them while your thoughts about your to-do list are still floating around, demanding your focus and attention. Has this happened to you? Maybe not this exact scenario but maybe your significant other is there trying to speak with you about something and you cannot pay full attention because of the attention suck of your to-do list?

That is because we live in a world of things that happened that we are worried about/concerned about/afraid of in the past or in the future. When that is occurring, it pulls us from life. We never learn to savor important moments. Our days become blurs, and we are suddenly a little older and feel like we have nothing to show for it.

When we go through life in this way, we are not living in a way that is fulfilling. In this modern age, our attention spans have gotten smaller. We look to our phones, laptops, televisions, or other external things to focus on instead of focusing on our lives.

You must learn to cultivate presence.

Have you ever gone on vacation and gotten sick? Is that a pattern in your life? Most high achievers are so busy that when they finally take a break, they get sick. We are filled with the next project, reaching out to work on other projects because we know we can fix them. Then, we find ourselves in overwhelm. We either get sick while on vacation because our bodies can finally relax, or we don't take enough vacation and get sick because our bodies cannot take anymore and force us to rest.

When you focus on your phone (which releases dopamine), you feel good. Then, you keep scrolling, swiping, and seeking that next rush—and you keep getting it. Next thing you know, you start feeling badly. There are studies on this behavior, and it is hard to break the addiction for many people. We have become social media dopamine addicts.

Worse, we learn to live our lives scrolling through someone else's. Basically, we are handing over our lives to others when we continue scrolling. We become watchers of someone else's life. The net result of your scrolling is that you train yourself to be entertained by something outside of yourself, which leads to addiction, and then the only thing you start talking about is what other people are doing in their lives. How is this living a fulfilled life?

Instead, cultivate presence and gratitude. When you learn to cultivate presence, you remember little moments, you savor time spent with your friends, you appreciate your kids and are present with them when spending time with them instead of having your head off in the clouds worrying about your to-do list.

But how?

Meditation helps you to focus. Many people start a practice and never follow through. People are so attention-deficient, more so now than ever before, that they cannot devote five minutes to sitting alone without thinking of picking up their phone, looking at their email, or anything else other than sitting quietly.

There are research-backed findings that indicate meditation's effectiveness on lowering blood pressure. The article does state that more evidence is needed, but preliminary findings are positive.

Brook RD, Appel RJ, Rubenfire M, et al. Beyond medications and diet: alternative approaches to lowering blood pressure: a scientific statement from the American Heart Association. Hypertension. 2013;61(6):1360–1383.

There are numerous studies that indicate meditation can reduce anxiety.

In addition, according to the National Center for Complementary and Integrative Health, "Some research suggests that practicing meditation may reduce blood pressure, symptoms of irritable bowel syndrome, anxiety and depression, and insomnia."[2]

The most interesting study is that meditation physically changes the brain. There was an eight-week study at the University of Massachusetts Medical School's Center for Mindfulness that showed evidence of brain changes after two months of daily meditation for thirty minutes each day. [3]

Why Do I Need to Meditate?

Meditation is a part of self-support. The Mayo Clinic says, "Meditation can give you a sense of calm, peace and balance that can benefit both your emotional well-being and your overall health. And these benefits don't end when your meditation session ends. Meditation can help carry you more calmly through your day and may help you manage symptoms of certain medical conditions."

The sense of being present does not happen immediately for most people. It takes time to change, to settle the mind, and to experience the calm that meditation leads to when practiced daily.

I remember sharing a quick calming technique with a client who came to me because she was overwhelmed. In the beginning, I asked her to take three deep breaths because I could see that she was agitated and couldn't focus. When I asked her to take three long, deep breaths, she took three shallow breaths in rapid succession and exclaimed, "It's not working!" Clearly, it was not working because she was not paying attention; she had not practiced being calm and had no belief she could calm herself down by simply breathing.

Eventually, she started to breathe as I had instructed, and she calmed down. But here is the secret sauce: practice breathing and calming down every day and you will be able to calm yourself down before it reaches that tipping point of feeling panicked.

When you conduct a daily meditation practice, you will find that you have an increased ability to calm yourself down more frequently. You develop focus and learn to not let your mind take you away from the time you spend with your family, kids, pets, friends, work, and life in general. When you are more present, you see life unfolding for you, not against you.

Volunteer

Volunteering is one of my favorite go-tos when people ask me about wanting to meet new friends or gain new experiences. When we give back to our communities, it helps us boost our social skills or even make new friends. It can also expand your network.

This act of giving also can help you develop a sense of purpose in life. When you help others, you might find this is your calling or at the very least, part of your calling in life. When we pave the way for others, we make our world a little brighter.

Find a cause that you are passionate about and go help. Learn about the organization that you are helping. One of the things I find to be a valuable way to gain experience is to volunteer. Our current jobs may not give us the opportunities we need to move to the next level, and we cannot get into the next level role without having experience. One way to overcome that is to volunteer to lead a team of people at a not-for-profit or to get a nomination to be on the board of your favorite local charity organization.

Many people find that they can gain critical skills needed for career advancement. Volunteering might give you those critical leadership skills you need to land that new job you've identified as one relating to your life's purpose/mission. As discussed in an earlier chapter, women often do not get onto the corporate ladder because there is a missing rung for many of us. Once on the ladder, we do not always get the same opportunities available to men.

According to CNBC, "Overall, women in corporate America are 24% less likely than men to get advice from senior leaders, according to a Lean In and SurveyMonkey study. And 62% of women of color say they believe a lack of mentorship holds them back in their career."[4]

Some ways to get around this phenomenon is to gain your experience externally by volunteerism. You might need to volunteer for a while before being able to get on the board and gain those much-needed skills, but make it known that is what you are seeking and meet the other board members to let them know. You can also do the same in your work environment to let senior leaders know that this is the direction you intend to go and ask for their advice.

In fact, many have made great strides in requesting meetings with senior leaders by simply asking them for a coffee chat. Make the goal of the meeting something along the lines of seeking career guidance so the purpose of the meeting is perfectly clear. Many people would welcome the opportunity to meet with you and share advice. Many folks have found sponsors by utilizing that method. It works in volunteer organizations as well.

If your life's purpose is to start a not-for-profit organization, having experience as a board member will give you deep insight into what is involved in that endeavor so you are better prepared. The other thing I would suggest is to look around and research to ensure there are no other existing not-for-profits that are doing what you're hoping to accomplish. If you find one that is already doing what you envision, then do everything you can to get involved in that organization and work to get on the board to help drive decisions that lead to greater success. There are many already existing not-for-profits that are struggling and could use your help. The advice in that scenario is to help them first unless your idea is revolutionary and unique. If so, go for it!

---

1. The Professional Counselor, "Self-Care Through Self-Compassion: A Balm for Burnout," https://files.eric.ed.gov/fulltext/EJ1165683.pdf

2. National Center for Complementary and Integrative Health, "Meditation and Mindfulness: What You Need to Know," https://www.nccih.nih.gov/health/meditation-in-depth

3. Mindworks, "What Happens to Your Mind, Brain and Body During Meditation?" https://mindworks.org/blog/what-happens-to-your-mind-brain-and-body-during-meditation/

4. CNBC Make It, "Ambition is not the problem: Women want the top jobs—they just don't get them," https://www.cnbc.com/2020/03/05/why-women-are-locked-out-of-top-jobs-despite-having-high-ambition.html

SECTION V: THE PLAY
TIPS FOR SUCCESSFUL GAME PLAY

CHAPTER 22
GRATITUDE

Have you ever looked at your child's face and at that moment felt such joy and gratitude for them? What about your dog, who every single day is so excited to see you when you come home—does that warm your heart? Those moments are irreplaceable. But we don't savor them or think about them very often. When these events happen, your heart opens and you feel wonderful. Those moments can create such a feeling of sereneness and contentedness that fills your very spirit.

Did you know you could bring that feeling into yourself every single day? Further, did you know that when you start your day off feeling those wonderful thoughts and feelings, it impacts your day for the better?

When reading those statements above, did you remember a time when you felt that joy and complete feeling of love? If not, take a few moments, close your eyes, and think of a time or moment when you were proud of something you did. It could be when you were a kid and you won that game, got your first A on an English paper, or when you graduated high school, had your first child, met your significant other, etc. Relive it. Imagine it happening. Feel how you felt.

Our minds are incredibly powerful and trigger feelings whether good or bad. Imagine biting into a lemon. Did your mouth just pucker when reading that statement? That is the power of our thoughts. They can create feelings—real or not real. Our brains don't care if it is real or not; just the thought conjured up a response in your body. For survival, our brains are continuously scanning our environment for something that might be wrong. Think about our ancestors in the wild, picking berries to eat. Their brains were developed in such a way as to scan automatically for any threats, like a large animal that might harm them. Well, our brains still work that way. As a result, imagine working in an office environment, your brain searches for some threat—perceived or real. Most of the time, it is perceived. You might think, *Oh, that group huddled across the hallway there, they must be talking about me.* Most of us don't jump to that particular conclusion, but the point still remains that we can assume threats that do not exist.

The problem is that if our brains are hard-wired to seek out only the bad and remember those bad things, then we remain in a constant state of negativity. Remember how we learned in an earlier chapter how our thoughts can quickly spiral us to a negative state of being? If our brains are geared to search the environment for only negative things and focus in on only those negative things, then we are already set up for a bad day. Then, our inner voices start to add to the pile of negativity. If someone says good morning, you might think to yourself, *What's so good about it?* It is easier to be unhappy because that is the normal outcome.

Psychologists refer to this phenomenon as negative bias or even it is sometimes called negativity bias. This negativity bias has a powerful effect on your behavior, the decisions you make, and even your relationships. Research shows that we remember more vividly the pain of a negative situation instead of the enjoyment of a positive one. That makes sense, right? If you ever touched a hot stove, you vividly recall that scenario and briefly might even relive the pain when describing it to others. But we rarely remember when we won that spelling bee that one year in fifth grade. The more deeply felt emotions from the burn are geared to prevent you from doing that action again. It is a survival technique.

The research indicates that we tend to remember traumatic events instead of positive ones. We also are more likely to remember negative feedback versus positive feedback in our performance reviews. Then, we stew on it which makes it even worse!

Think about a time when you were having a great day, and someone made an offhanded remark about your presentation from earlier in the day. Instead of being happy and proud of the work you did and the positive reception you got from the audience, you focus on this one comment, and it brings you into a downward spiral because you just cannot believe that this person would say such a thing. Further, when you meet someone later in the day, and they ask how you are doing, you say "terrible" and vent about the incident instead of thinking about all the positive things that happened, which outweigh that one negative comment.

Helping ourselves to remember the good things that happen every day is a proven method to ensure we capture all the great things we actually accomplished in a given day. Some people call this a gratitude journal. I call it a "swank bank!" It is important to capture all the accomplishments—big or small so that our negativity bias doesn't take over. This practice helps us remember that we did many great things instead of the one bad thing that happened that we typically place all of our attention on. So, when we get down in the dumps and feel like we haven't done much, reviewing everything you have accomplished is a great pick-me-up. Getting into this practice of capturing all the accomplishments helps you when you are updating your resume, preparing for a meeting with your boss at the end of the year, making a case for a promotion or salary increase, and more.

Journaling is also a great way to have an outlet for your thoughts and feelings. The act of writing down feelings enables us to get the thoughts from our heads onto paper, where we can then reflect upon them. Having a practice of writing daily accomplishments might also open the door to writing down your thoughts and feelings. Creating a daily practice helps us stay on track. For example, journaling can help us capture our daily successes to remember all the great things we have accomplished. It also gives us a much-needed outlet for writing out any unresolved feelings from the day. In fact, many people who find their minds spinning about the events from the day find it helpful to journal. Once all the thoughts are down on paper, our minds can relax, and many people find it easier to fall asleep afterward. It is important to help us uncover unresolved feelings from the day. Journaling is a great way to do that.

There may be times when you do not feel like writing anything in your journal. Rather than giving up the practice, take a break from writing about your successes or do not write anything at all for that day. If you ever feel pressured to write, then it is not helping you to do so. Look, sometimes we have trouble getting from the bed to the bathroom. Forget about writing anything down on those days. Let those days pass by, and when ready, go back and resume journaling. Sometimes, even just documenting those darker days will help you track how often you have them and maybe help you uncover trends that might be happening around the times when they occur. I have taken a piece of paper, written only the date, and said, "Not today." I folded up the paper to stick in the journal to record that I acknowledged the day but was not able or willing to write anything. By taking this action, I recorded the day but did not use up the pages in my journal. You will find your own techniques over time. But being able to go back and see how many days it lasted or being able to go back to that time and think about what might have been the root cause can sometimes be helpful. I wanted to make certain to share that because life happens. Let us be honest with ourselves and acknowledge that it happens.

When I notice I am not journaling, entering the daily entries, writing out my thoughts and reasons for being grateful, and not taking the time out for self-support, then I know I have fallen off track, and I must go back to journaling to figure out why this is happening. I do not like to go back and do the things needed. I would rather just tell myself, "I am okay, and I don't really need to write anything in that journal today, and I will exercise/meditate/sleep later. And this one piece of candy isn't hurting anyone…" The idea is that you track what you are doing to 1) get your feelings out and on paper, 2) write about what happened that is triggering those feelings, 3) determine how you might handle things differently or think about the thing that happened and reflect, and 4) when you are not writing in your journal and you see that you are not following your mission, ask yourself, "What am I avoiding?" or other prompts that will help you figure out what is going on and to get yourself back on track.

Think about the news. If it is negative, it sells. Even worse, when you watch the news repeatedly, you think the entire world is falling apart and start to view things more negatively. Many people turn off the news as a result of the continuous stream of negative events as a way to protect themselves from fear.

This negativity bias can also impact our relationships. Have you ever already put your defenses up on high alert because you assumed your significant other would react in a certain way, and you were thinking about it before you even say anything? Your thoughts assumed that you already knew how this was going to go, raising your blood pressure, making yourself angrier and angrier. Then, you finally tell your spouse the thing you needed to share, and he or she says, "Okay, that's fine." And all that worry, fear, and anger you built up in your head were for nothing. But it isn't "nothing," after all. You spiked your anger, and you already feel it in your body. According to an article printed in *Psychology Today*:

> "The body takes about 20 minutes to return to normal after a full fight/flight response. In other words, angry people need time to calm down before they can think clearly again. Angry people will not completely comprehend any explanations, solutions, or problem-solving options until their body returns to normal again."[1]

However, when you allow anger to take over, your body releases adrenaline, and that can take up to an hour to dissipate. This behavior can lead to headaches, heart problems, high blood pressure, or worse. Therefore, it is important to pay attention and remember you have a choice.

To counteract that hardwiring and automatic negativity, we need to learn how to re-train our thoughts to be more positive. The quickest way to do that is to practice gratitude.

You may be wondering, *Why gratitude?* To answer that question, consider Harvard Medical School's explanation, "Gratitude is a thankful appreciation for what an individual receives, whether tangible or intangible. With gratitude, people acknowledge the goodness in their lives...gratitude helps people feel more positive emotions, relish good experiences, improve their health, deal with adversity, and build strong relationships."[2]

Why are we all not doing this right now?

It takes work to go against your brain's auto programming. Most people are not even aware of this information and do not know how to overcome it or where to even start.

There is a course offered by Yale University Called "The Science of Well-Being." Over 3.4 million people enrolled as of the date I am writing this book. The course description states, "In this course, you will engage in a series of challenges designed to increase your own happiness and build more productive habits. As preparation for these tasks, Professor Laurie Santos reveals misconceptions about happiness, annoying features of the mind that lead us to think the way we do, and the research that can help us change. You will ultimately be prepared to successfully incorporate a specific wellness activity into your life."

I have taken the course and can tell you that there are a lot of misconceptions about happiness, and the truth based on research is eye-opening. For instance, I learned that the more you utilize the strengths that you inherently have, the more your happiness goes up (Hazer & Ruch, 2012). Like any good thing that you might get too much of (think of too much sunlight – it could result in a sunburn), there is a happy medium where it is best if you use four of the top seven strengths.

There is a lot of emphasis in this course on gratitude, and I would like to focus your attention on the reasons why gratitude is so important to overall mental health and wellbeing.

The professor goes into detail about savoring the moments that make you happy. Others will say to feel the joy, the taste, the smell, and all the feelings at that moment, and doing so helps you to savor the memory. Once we do that, we are connected emotionally to that moment, and then when we are thankful to have had the moment, it brings happiness over time and we feel less depressed.

Berkeley did a study with ~300 adults that were seeking counseling at the university. They divided the participants into three groups and asked one of the three groups to write gratitude letters. The results speak for themselves: "… those who wrote gratitude letters reported significantly better mental health four weeks and twelve weeks after their writing exercise ended. These results suggest that gratitude writing can be beneficial for healthy, well-adjusted individuals and those who struggle with mental health concerns. In fact, it seems that practicing gratitude alongside receiving psychological counseling carries greater benefits than counseling alone, even when that gratitude practice is brief."[3]

The team went on to find other key elements reflecting "how gratitude might actually work on our minds and bodies."

The most interesting finding was when they used an fMRI scanner to measure before and aftereffects. The act of gratitude writing had the largest impact on the medial prefrontal cortex three months after letter writing ended!

Another way in which gratitude helps, according to Hey Sigmund.com, is that it "…has the capacity to increase important neurochemicals. When thinking shifts from negative to positive, there is a surging of feel-good chemicals such as dopamine, serotonin, and oxytocin. These all contribute to the feelings of closeness, connection, and happiness that come with gratitude."[4]

In fact, one study showed that those who felt grateful had a noticeably reduced the stress hormone, cortisol. They even were "…more resilient to emotional setbacks and negative experiences." (cited in McCraty & Childre, 2004)

"Significant studies over the years have established the fact that by practicing gratitude we can handle stress better than others. By merely acknowledging and appreciating the little things in life, we can rewire the brain to deal with the present circumstances with more awareness and broader perception."[5]

The bottom line is that the physical act of embarking on the act of gratitude writing will improve your well-being.

How Do I Get Started with Gratitude?

Purchase a spiral notebook and create a space for writing the things for which you are grateful as you start the day and again as you end your day. One of the things I learned was to truly embrace the things for which you are grateful. Go back to and sit in the moment in time when the memory occurred. Take time to savor the feelings, allow them into your heart, and smell, see, and feel the feelings that took place during that event in your life as you write or shortly before. When you savor that emotional connection, it triggers all the positive emotions in your body and actually improves your mood.

Everything is a practice. It must be cultivated and doesn't happen overnight. You must remember to consistently put the practice of gratitude into a daily habit.

Once you do, your world changes. Happiness increases, you remember to be more present in the moment, and you relish your day instead of being a zombie that sleepwalks through life.

---

1. Psychology Today, "Controlling Angry People," https://www.psychologyto day.com/us/blog/let-their-words-do-the-talking/201101/controlling-angry-people
2. Harvard Health Publishing, "Giving Thanks Can Make You Happier," https://www.health.harvard.edu/healthbeat/giving-thanks-can-make-you-happier
3. Greater Good Magazine, "How Gratitude Changes You and Your Brain," https://greatergood.berkeley.edu/article/item/how_gratitude_changes_you_and_your_brain
4. Hey Sigmund, "The Science of Gratitude – How it Changes People, Relationships (and Brains!) and How to Make it Work For You," https://www.heysig mund.com/the-science-of-gratitude/
5. Positive Psychology, "The Neuroscience of Gratitude and How It Affects Anxiety & Grief," https://positivepsychology.com/neuroscience-of-gratitude/

CHAPTER 23
FEAR

It can be intimidating when you look at this journal and you are afraid to write anything in it. You might end up feeling guilty because you do not feel that you can write in it today. Then, you walk away and go to your habit of choice: the candy jar, the pantry, a cigarette, a drink, or whatever your numbing habit happens to be that takes away the feelings (momentarily). I am here to tell you to put that journal down. Take three deep breaths, count backward from five, and get a piece of paper. Before you go to the numbing habit of choice, you can take a minute and write down on that paper what feelings came up for you just then. What made you afraid? What caused the feelings. For me, it took me a lot of practice to even be able to identify my feelings. For those of you like me, print out this feeling wheel at www.feel ingswheel.com or search for it using those terms and find one that works for you. There are tons of them like this online, so find one where the feelings are listed for you to identify. Pinpoint what you feel on the wheel. Honor your feeling. Realize that you are experiencing this feeling or these feelings, and it means that you are human. You are okay. Feelings are part of who we are. If you feel angry, work your way on the wheel to get more clarification on what that means exactly. Does it feel like disrespectful anger or infuriated anger? There are a few different terms that you might find come closer to the overall angry feeling you have.

The point of this exercise is to recognize and realize what your body is telling you. If you feel angry and then look at the wheel and agree that frustrated is a little more accurate and then you get down to the feeling of being infuriated, it might help you pinpoint the most descriptive term, which then, in turn, might help you realize what happened, or what memory triggered that/those emotions. This wheel has helped me accurately sit with and learn from my feelings. Maybe this is not an issue for you, but it helped me, and I wanted to include it for anyone else it might help.

It is important to tell yourself you give yourself permission to feel these feelings. Often, when we run to something to numb the pain, we are trying to prevent these feelings from coming out. Therefore, forcing yourself to take three deep breaths and then slowly count backward from five can give you a breather and help you think about maybe another choice instead of the one you were going to when you were on autopilot. If you NEED that numbing habit, give yourself permission. But do your best to try to sit with your feelings. I would write furiously about all the things associated with the feelings, like slamming the pen on the paper hard and writing fast and angrily to get the feelings out. You might not need to write like that but if you do, keep going. You are getting it out of your head and on paper and it might take the edge off without the numbing habit.

If you do decide you can wait some more before going to the numbing habit, go for a walk, take a bath, turn on some music, or do something else that is soothing to you that is a more positive alternative. Once you calm down, go back to thinking about the feelings that came up. It might be the same day or the next, but go back when you are able. What were the feelings? What caused the feelings to surface? What were the circumstances? Honor the feelings and honor the fact that you had to numb this out because you did not want to face it. It was a protection mechanism. Hug yourself and thank yourself for being human and feeling something. Thank yourself for allowing the feelings to surface. The goal here is to recognize something that came up that triggered you to want to go to that habit. Look at the feeling or feelings and sit with them. Identify them and journal the feelings and circumstances. This process releases the feelings from your mind and places them on paper.

If this process starts to be overwhelming, do not continue. Reach out to a therapist or work with one to help you if the feelings are not manageable.

If they are and you feel confident about moving forward, write down action steps you can put into place. Let me give you an example of how I went through something recently and used this process to get through the issue. I was not listening to someone at work in a meeting in front of others. It was not me at my highest or best, but I am being honest. I am far from perfect, but the process does work. I realized I felt terrible afterward because I was actually resentful. I shut down my listening because I was not going to hear what this person was saying to me. The truth of the matter is that I was triggered by the path the speaker was going down. It did not lead to where I assumed it was going. The speaker went into a different topic, but my feelings of resentment came flying out and shut down my ability to concentrate or hear what the person was actually saying. I felt horrible afterward.

I went through the process and realized what I did. I acknowledged my feelings and took action steps to apologize later to the speaker.

Again, not proud of that moment. But it is important to share how our subconscious can take over and cause reactions that are unwarranted. They sometimes are warranted, so being able to discern takes practice and really working through those uncomfortable things that we usually don't want to do. It helps us grow in the long run.

This is a truth journey. If I cannot be honest with myself, then I am just a dispenser, not a helper. Make the investment in your soul. You are worth it.

Here is another method of helping yourself remember what you have done and to recognize that you have truly good qualities.

Answer the following questions:

What Has Made Me Really Happy in My Life?

List as many of those moments as you can. It could be a simple "thank you" someone said for something you did all the way up to your wedding day. Keep writing them down on paper and keep this paper.

I Am Proud of…

Listing out things that you are proud of, things you have accomplished, or achievements that took some doing to attain are the types of things that help us remember all the things we have accomplished in our lives. It helps to strengthen us. Write down as many as you can think of.

What Makes You YOU?

What unique aspects do you have that make you who you are? I love to learn and always had my head in a book or was taking a class or going to a lecture series. I learned to love that aspect of me. What are some of your unique qualities that you can celebrate?

What Do Your Co-Workers Say About You?

Now, this question can put an insecure person right into fear. But try not to let that happen. Ask a co-worker to share what they think you are good at doing. Pick someone who is more of a friend. Listen to what they say and write it down. If no one at work seems like they would be willing to share their thoughts with you, ask your friends or even family members.

Okay, now you have a list of things that make you happy, that others have said you are good at doing, and things that you are proud of. Keep this list handy and when your self-doubts pop up, remember to refer to this list. Keep it in your journal. If it is there in the journal you can use and refer to every day to remind yourself about your unique talents and gifts. Remembering these good qualities you possess helps you to overcome those self-doubts. In fact, many people start out their day, after writing down all the things for which they are grateful, by remembering these things about themselves. This gets them ready to face the day with a smile and with the knowledge that they can do it! They have done things in the past that made them feel proud, and they have confidence that they can reach their goals.

Remember, fear is normal for everyone. Most of us push through our fears even though we are afraid. But there are certain circumstances where we just cannot seem to move past our fears. For example, public speaking for some is fearful. Joining a local speech giving club like Toastmasters can help most people but for some, they cannot get past it. I always advise clients to think about a time when they were afraid, but they kept moving forward anyway. Hold onto that memory and be proud of it. When you find yourself being afraid of moving forward (use your feelings wheel to identify which aspect of fear you might be feeling), pull that memory from your memory bank and savor it. Relish in the way you kept moving forward and remember how you felt and the joy at the success you achieve. Even if it is a small victory, relish it. The memory and the feelings you generate will help you push through the fears you are facing or will be facing in the future.

> *"Thinking will not overcome fear, but action will."*
> —W. Clement Stone

CHAPTER 24
CONCLUSION

Before you go, here is a recap of steps. This reference guide will make the steps easier to follow. You can get this checklist on my website (plus find lots more information like videos and articles on this topic) by visiting:

www.kennedyeffect.com/downloads

Find Your Life's Purpose/Mission

1. Write down as many ideas of things/interests that are your passion, things that cause a spark for you.
2. Prioritize top one or two.
3. Apply the 5 Whys Approach.
4. Is it still valid? If "yes," move to step 5. If "no," go back and choose another area of interest and repeat.
5. Once you know your area of passion and have a statement ready, that becomes your mission statement. For example, I want to make people happy.

How Will You Achieve Your Mission?

How do you want to make them happy? You might start with something like writing books, writing music, baking them delicious muffins, etc. Write what you feel you are most passionate about.

Goals:

1. Then, start writing down a few goals that you want to accomplish that are related to your Mission statement. Say, for example, you wanted to bake. Your goals might be: 1) Start baking muffins to sell at a flea market. 2) Start selling baked goods to stores. 3) Have a food truck that offers all kinds of baked goods.
2. Pick one of the goals and build out the steps you would need to take to achieve that goal. Is it manageable? Is it reasonable? How long will it take to achieve it? Check your mission statement again—is it aligned? Do you feel passionate about the goal you set?
3. Create a timeline for each step (make a start date and another column for end date). As you look at all these steps, is anything missing?
4. Are there any risks to your plan that you can think of that might get in the way? Write them down. Then, write down the ways in which you would mitigate the risk.
5. Map those start dates and ends dates in your monthly planner. Then, for the upcoming week, write out the things you need to get done for the week. Identify on which days during the week you will work on those tasks. It might be one task that you do for several days (or if writing a book, several months!).

6. On the day you start, begin in the morning by filling out your planner. Remind yourself what the mission is and the overarching strategy—for example, I want to bake muffins. When you look at that day, you are reminded of what you said you wanted to accomplish and why.

7. Self-Support Exercise: Be sure to think about the things you will do for breaks—exercise, a walk, meditation, yoga stretch, etc. Think about what you can do for a quick ten minutes, schedule in your thirty-minute block, and then schedule the forty-five to sixty-minute session.

8. Answer the questions around eating well. Are you eating the right foods and fueling your body?

9. DISCIPLINE! Remember your "why" and focus on not letting anything distract you from moving forward. You got this!

I cannot wait to hear about the successes that you will accomplish as a result of following this system and using the journal. Please write to me at: pkennedy@kennedyeffect.com to keep me apprised of your progress and success. You can also join my free Facebook Group:

Women Creating Dream Careers!

Find us at https://www.facebook.com/groups/345676177023098.

And please visit my web page for the most up-to-date free resources, blogs, and videos to help you move forward.

www.Kennedyeffect.com

I wish all the best for you as you begin this journey to create your own rules in the Game of Life! Please keep in touch and let me know how you are rewriting your Game of Life plans!

ABOUT THE AUTHOR

I simplify the complexities of self-help. Knowing what the Game of Life template could be (your destination goals and the steps to get there), I bridge the gaps to show you what might be missing. That way, you can connect the dots and create the strategy you need for success in the Game of Life!

My passion is empowering others to learn their mission and what they aspire to be in their lives and then make plans accordingly. I want to help people find their life's purpose and help them create goals to ensure they reach their vision.

As an Experienced Women in Leadership coach for Fortune 150 companies, I've used my expertise to empower clients to fulfill their life and career goals. My mentorship programs deliver results. Many of the participants of my program earn promotions within one year of completion—a high achievement. I've been humbled to learn that my coaching for sales teams resulted in record-breaking performance outcomes.

You can find me kicking my kids' butts at board games, hiking, or taking long walks with my family when I'm not working. I love painting, listening to murder mystery podcasts while getting my steps in, curling up in a blanket with a good book, and solving an escape room puzzle with friends.

REFERENCES

"4 Pillars of Hinduism."
https://www.bbc.co.uk/bitesize/guides/zmvhsrd/
revision/2#:~:text=The%20purpose%20of%20life%20-
for,and%20lead%20a%20good%20life.

"11 Facts about Teens and Self Esteem." DoSomething.org.
Accessed August 1, 2022. https://www.dosomething.org/us/
facts/11-facts-about-teens-and-self-esteem.

"16 Personalities Test." 16Personalities. Accessed August 1, 2022.
https://www.16personalities.com/.

Ackerman , Courtney E. "83 Benefits of Journaling for Depression,
Anxiety, and Stress." PositivePsychology.com, May 14, 2018.
https://positivepsychology.com/benefits-of-journaling/.

"The Act of Smiling." SOVA, June 3, 2019. https://sova.pitt.edu/
be-positive-the-act-of-smiling.

Babcock, Linda, Maria P. Reclade, and Lise Vesterlund. "Why Women Volunteer for Tasks That Don't Lead to Promotions." *Harvard Business Review,* July 16, 2018. https://hbr.org/2018/07/why-women-volunteer-for-tasks-that-dont-lead-to-promotions.

Barr, Sabrina. "Women Are Still Doing the Majority of Household Chores, Study Finds." The Independent. Independent Digital News and Media, July 26, 2019. https://www.independent.co.uk/life-style/women-men-household-chores-domestic-house-gender-norms-a9021586.html.

Barroso, Amanda, and Anna Brown. "Gender Pay Gap in U.S. Held Steady in 2020." Pew Research Center. Pew Research Center, June 8, 2022. https://www.pewresearch.org/fact-tank/2021/05/25/gender-pay-gap-facts/.

Bassi, Marina, Mercedes Mateo Díaz, Rae Lesser Blumberg, and Ana Reynoso. "Failing to Notice? Uneven Teachers' Attention to Boys and Girls in the Classroom - IZA Journal of Labor Economics." SpringerOpen. Springer Berlin Heidelberg, November 13, 2018. https://izajole.springeropen.com/articles/10.1186/s40172-018-0069-4.

Bernstein, Elizabeth. "Ways to Say 'No' More Effectively." *The Wall Street Journal.* Dow Jones & Company, March 10, 2014. https://www.wsj.com/articles/SB10001424052702303795904579431093572107898.

Bhattacharya, Shaoni. "Women Marry Men Who Look like Dad." *New Scientist.* New Scientist, April 27, 2004. https://www.newscientist.com/article/dn4928-women-marry-men-who-look-like-dad/.

Bittner, Ashley, and Brigette Lau. "Women-Led Startups Received Just 2.3% of VC Funding in 2020." *Harvard Business Review*, February 21, 2021. https://hbr.org/2021/02/women-led-startups-received-just-2-3-of-vc-funding-in-2020.

"Brainfacts." BrainFacts.org. Accessed August 1, 2022. https://www.brainfacts.org/.

Brook, Robert D., Lawrence J. Appel, Melvyn Rubenfire, Gbenga Ogedegbe, John D. Bisognano, William J. Elliott, Flavio D. Fuchs, et al. "Beyond Medications and Diet: Alternative Approaches to Lowering Blood Pressure." *Hypertension* 61, no. 6 (2013): 1360–83. https://doi.org/10.1161/hyp.0b013e318293645f.

Brown, James, and Betty Jean Newsome. "It's a Man's Man's Man's World." 1966.

Brown, Joshua, and Joel Wong. "How Gratitude Changes You and Your Brain." Greater Good, June 6, 2017. https://greatergood.berkeley.edu/article/item/how_gratitude_changes_you_and_your_brain.

Canfield, Jack. *The Success Principles*. HarperCollins Publishers, 2004.

Carnegie, Dale. *How to Win Friends and Influence People*. 1st ed. Simon & Schuster, 1936.

Cassata, Cathy. "The Benefits of Emotional Intelligence (EQ) at Work." Psych Central. Psych Central, September 27, 2021. https://psychcentral.com/blog/the-benefits-of-emotional-intelligence#1.

Cherry, Kendra. "Why Our Brains Are Hardwired to Focus on the

Negative." Verywell Mind. Verywell Mind, April 29, 2020. https://www.verywellmind.com/negative-bias-4589618. Chowdhury, Madhuleena Roy. "The Neuroscience of Gratitude and How It Affects Anxiety & Grief." PositivePsychology.com, April 9, 2019. https://positivepsychology.com/neuroscience-of-gratitude/.

Clay, Rebecca A. "Just Say No." American Psychological Association. American Psychological Association. Accessed August 1, 2022. https://www.apa.org/gradpsych/2013/11/say-no.

Clear, James. *Atomic Habits: An Easy & Proven Way to Build Good Habits & Break Bad Ones.* Avery Publishing Group, 2018.
Clifton, Donald O. *Now, Discover Your Strengths: The Revolutionary Gallup Program That Shows You How to Develop Your Unique Talents and Strengths.* New York: Gallup Press, 2020.

Coaston, Susannah C. "Self-Care through Self-Compassion: A Balm for Burnout." *The Professional Counselor*, 2017. https://files.eric.ed.gov/fulltext/EJ1165683.pdf.
Connley, Courtney. "Ambition Is Not the Problem: Women Want the Top Jobs-They Just Don't Get Them." CNBC. CNBC, March 5, 2020. https://www.cnbc.com/2020/03/05/why-women-are-locked-out-of-top-jobs-despite-having-high-ambition.html.

Covey, Stephen R. *The 7 Habits of Highly Effective People.* New York: Free Press, 2004.

Cronometer is a trademark of Cronometer Software Inc.

Cyrus, Miley, Jessi Alexander, and Jon Mabe. "The Climb." MP3. John Shanks. 2009.

Derbyshire, Jon. "The BA Skill Set – 5 Whys Technique."

LinkedIn. LinkedIn, June 25, 2018. https://www.linkedin.com/pulse/ba-skill-set-5-whys-technique-jon-derbyshire/.

"The Eisenhower Matrix." The Decision Lab. Accessed August 1, 2022. https://thedecisionlab.com/reference-guide/management/the-eisenhower-matrix.

Excel is a trademark of Microsoft Corporation.

"FAQs." Meta - Resources. Accessed August 1, 2022. https://investor.fb.com/resources/default.aspx.

Farber, Sharon K. "Expressive Writing for Physical and Mental Health." Psychology Today. Sussex Publishers, March 28, 2016. https://www.psychologytoday.com/us/blog/the-mind-body-connection/201603/expressive-writing-physical-and-mental-health.

Finding Nemo. United States: Walt Disney Pictures, 2003.

Fortune 500 is a trademark of Fortune Media IP Limited.

Friedman, Mike. *Hardcore Humanism*. 2021.

Gardner, Sarah, and Dave Albee. "Study Focuses on Strategies for Achieving Goals ... - Dominican Scholar." Dominican University of California, February 1, 2015. https://scholar.dominican.edu/cgi/viewcontent.cgi?article=1265&context=news-releases.

Girl Scouts is a trademark of Girl Scouts of the United States of America.

"Giving Thanks Can Make You Happier." Harvard Health,

August 14, 2021. https://www.health.harvard.edu/healthbeat/ giving-thanks-can-make-you-happier.

Hasseldine, Rosjke. "Why Do Women Find It so Difficult to Put Themselves First?" *HuffPost*. HuffPost, June 22, 2016. https:// www.huffpost.com/entry/why-do-women-find-it-so- d_b_7621976.

Hewlett, Sylvia Ann. *Forget a Mentor, Find a Sponsor: The New Way to Fast-Track Your Career*. Harvard Business Review Press, 2013.

Holmes, Ryan. "The Elephant and the Rope: One Mental Trick to Unlock Your Growth." Inc.com. Inc., January 30, 2017. https:// www.inc.com/ryan-holmes/the-elephant-and-the-rope-one- mental-trick-to-unlock-your-growth.html.

Horvath, Julia. "How to Set Healthy Boundaries-A Compassionate Guide for Women." *Medium*. Better Humans, February 10, 2021. https://betterhumans.pub/how-to-set-healthy-boundaries- a-compassionate-guide-for-women-98a509d853a8.

Howes, Ryan. "Give a Man a Fish…" Psychology Today. Sussex Publishers, May 7, 2008. https://www.psychologytoday.com/us/ blog/in-therapy/200805/give-man-fish.

"ICF, the Gold Standard in Coaching: Read about ICF." International Coaching Federation, May 20, 2022. https://coach ingfederation.org/about.

Ignatova, Maria. "New Report: Women Apply to Fewer Jobs than Men, but Are More Likely to Get Hired." LinkedIn, 2019. https:// www.linkedin.com/business/talent/blog/talent-acquisition/ how-women-find-jobs-gender-report.

Inc. "Cliftonstrengths." Gallup.com. Gallup, July 16, 2022. https://www.gallup.com/cliftonstrengths/en/252137/home.aspx.

Jones, Janelle. "5 Facts about the State of the Gender Pay Gap." United States Department of Labor, March 19, 2021. https://blog.dol.gov/2021/03/19/5-facts-about-the-state-of-the-gender-pay-gap.

"Journaling for Mental Health." University of Rochester Medical Center. Accessed August 1, 2022. https://www.urmc.rochester.edu/encyclopedia/content.aspx?ContentID=4552&ContentTypeID=1.

Kaufman, Scott Barry. "Who Created Maslow's Iconic Pyramid?" Scientific American Blog Network. Scientific American, April 23, 2019. https://blogs.scientificamerican.com/beautiful-minds/who-created-maslows-iconic-pyramid/.

Khosroshahi, Hanieh. "The Concrete Ceiling (SSIR)." Women of Color's Struggle Against Racism Is Revealed by the 'Concrete Ceiling', May 10, 2021. https://ssir.org/articles/entry/the_concrete_ceiling.

Kim, Jae Yun, Troy H. Campbell, Steven Shepherd, and Aaron C. Kay. "Understanding Contemporary Forms of Exploitation: Attributions of Passion Serve to Legitimize the Poor Treatment of Workers." *Journal of Personality and Social Psychology*. U.S. National Library of Medicine. Accessed August 1, 2022. https://pubmed.ncbi.nlm.nih.gov/30998042/.

Klaus, Peggy. *Brag! The Art of Tooting Your Own Horn Without Blowing It*. Warner Business Books, 2003.

Kreamer, Anne. "Not Taking Risks Is the Riskiest Career Move of All." Harvard Business Review, April 16, 2015. https://hbr.org/2015/04/not-taking-risks-is-the-riskiest-career-move-of-all.

Leinwand, Laurie. "How Journaling Heals: There's No 'Write' Way to Journal." GoodTherapy.org Therapy Blog, January 11, 2016. https://www.goodtherapy.org/blog/how-journaling-heals-theres-no-write-way-to-journal-0111155.

LinkedIn is a trademark of LinkedIn Corporation.

Maslow's Hierarchy of Needs: https://blogs.scientificamerican.com/beautiful-minds/who-created-maslows-iconic-pyramid/

McCraty, Rollin, and Doc Childre. "The Grateful Heart." *The Psychology of Gratitude*, 2004, 230–56. https://doi.org/10.1093/acprof:oso/9780195150100.003.0012.

Mcleod, Saul. "Maslow's Hierarchy of Needs." *Simply Psychology*, 2007. https://www.simplypsychology.org/maslow.html.

"Meditation and Mindfulness: What You Need to Know." National Center for Complementary and Integrative Health. U.S. Department of Health and Human Services. Accessed August 1, 2022. https://www.nccih.nih.gov/health/meditation-and-mindfulness-what-you-need-to-know.

"Meditation: A Simple, Fast Way to Reduce Stress." Mayo Clinic. Mayo Foundation for Medical Education and Research, April 29, 2022. https://www.mayoclinic.org/tests-procedures/meditation/in-depth/meditation/art-20045858.

Meta is a trademark of Facebook.

Microsoft Teams is a trademark of Microsoft Corporation.

Monopoly is a trademark of Hasbro, Inc.

Newman, Kira M. "How Journaling Can Help You in Hard Times." Greater Good, August 18, 2020. https://greatergood. berkeley.edu/article/item/how_journaling_can_help_y ou_in_hard_times.

Nine to Five. Directed by Colin Higgins, performances Jane Fonda, Lily Tomlin, and Dolly Parton, IPC Films, 1980.

Orzabal, Roland. "Mad World." Tears for Fears, *The Hurting*, 1982.

Peters, Julie. "Writing to Connect to Your Body." Spirituality & Health, December 10, 2015. https://www.spiritualityhealth.com/ blogs/pathfinding-yoga-and-mindfulness/2015/12/10/julie-peters-writing-connect-your-body.

Plato. *The Republic.* Createspace Independent Publishing Platform, 2019.

Polard, Andrea F. "Help, I Married My Father." Psychology Today. Sussex Publishers, July 27, 2017. https://www.psychologytoday. com/us/blog/unified-theory-happiness/201707/help-i-married-my-father.

Tesla is a trademark of Tesla, Inc.

"The Purpose of Life - Hindu Beliefs - Edexcel - GCSE Religious Studies Revision - Edexcel - BBC Bitesize." BBC News. BBC. Accessed August 1, 2022. https://www.bbc.co.uk/bitesize/ guides/zmvhsrd/revision/2#:~:text=The%20pur-pose%20of%20life%20for,and%20lead%20a%20good%20life.

"A Quote by Albert Einstein." Goodreads. Goodreads. Accessed August 1, 2022. https://www.goodreads.com/quotes/11458-i-have-no-special-talents-i-am-only-passionately-curious.

"A Quote by Antoine De Saint-Exupéry." Goodreads. Goodreads. Accessed August 1, 2022. https://www.goodreads.com/quotes/87476-a-goal-without-a-plan-is-just-a-wish.

"A Quote by B.B. King." Goodreads. Goodreads. Accessed August 1, 2022. https://www.goodreads.com/quotes/833-the-beautiful-thing-about-learning-is-nobody-can-take-it.

"Resources." The Kennedy Effect. Accessed August 1, 2022. https://www.kennedyeffect.com/website-resources.

Rodsky, Eve. *Fair Play: A Game-Changing Solution for When You Have Too Much to Do (and More Life to Live)*. New York: G.P. Putnam's Sons, 2019.

"Salary Data and Insights for Employers." Salary data and insights for employers | Randstad USA, August 10, 2021. https://www.randstadusa.com/business/salary-insights/?utm_campaign=rusa_Salary%2BGuide%2B2020_client_rus_all&%3Butm_medium=press&%3Butm_source=prnewswire.

Schafer, Jack. "Controlling Angry People." Psychology Today. Sussex Publishers, January 5, 2011. https://www.psychologytoday.com/us/blog/let-their-words-do-the-talking/201101/controlling-angry-people.

"The Science of Well-Being." Coursera. Accessed August 2, 2022. https://www.coursera.org/learn/the-science-of-well-being.

Shark Tank. 2009 to present. Produced by Mark Burnett Productions (2009–11), One Three Media (2012–14), United Artists Media Group (2014–15), MGM Television (2016–), Sony Pictures Television Studios.

Simonds, David. "Tesla Mission Statement 2022: Tesla Mission & Vision Analysis." What is Company Mission Statement? | Difference Between Mission & Vision, January 27, 2021. https://mission-statement.com/tesla/.

"Sleep and Mental Health - Harvard Health Publishing." Harvard Health, August 17, 2021. https://www.health.harvard.edu/newsletter_article/sleep-and-mental-health.

Smith, Jessi L., and Meghan Huntoon. "Women's Bragging Rights: Overcoming Modesty Norms to Facilitate Women's Self-Promotion." Sage Pub. Sage Journals, December 20, 2013. https://journals.sagepub.com/doi/10.1177/0361684313515840?icid=int.sj-abstract.similar-articles.1&.

"Study Explores Professional Mentor-Mentee Relationships in 2019." Olivet Nazarene University, 2019. https://online.olivet.edu/research-statistics-on-professional-mentors.

TED Talks is a trademark of Ted Conferences, LLC.

Toastmasters is a trademark of Toastmasters International.

Tulshyan, Ruchika, and Jodi-Ann Burey. "Stop Telling Women They Have Imposter Syndrome." *Harvard Business Review,* February 11, 2021. https://hbr.org/2021/02/stop-telling-women-they-have-imposter-syndrome.

"Veda." Oxford Reference. Accessed August 4, 2022. https://

www.oxfordreference.com/view/10.1093/oi/authority.
20110803115340387.

"W. Clement Stone Quotes." BrainyQuote. Xplore. Accessed
August 2, 2022. https://www.brainyquote.com/quotes/
w_clement_stone_155728.

Weir, Kirsten. "Feel like a Fraud?" American Psychological Association. American Psychological Association. Accessed August 1,
2022. https://www.apa.org/gradpsych/2013/11/fraud.

"What Happens to Your Mind, Brain & Body during Meditation?:
Mindworks." Mindworks Meditation. Accessed August 1, 2022.
https://mindworks.org/blog/what-happens-to-your-mind-brain-
and-body-during-meditation/.

"What's the Cost of the Mind-Body Connection?" Johns Hopkins
HealthCare Solutions, February 11, 2020. https://www.johnshop
kinssolutions.com/cost-of-the-mind-body-connection/.

"Women in the Workplace 2019." NEW REPORT: Women in the
Workplace 2019, 2019. https://womenintheworkplace.com/2019.

"Women in the Workplace 2021." McKinsey & Company.
McKinsey & Company, April 13, 2022. https://www.mckinsey.
com/featured-insights/diversity-and-inclusion/women-in-the-
workplace.

Young, Karen. "The Science of Gratitude - How It Changes People,
Relationships (and Brains!) and How to Make It Work for You."
Hey Sigmund, October 15, 2020. https://www.heysigmund.com/
the-science-of-gratitude/.

"Your Body Language May Shape Who You Are." Amy Cuddy:

Your body language may shape who you are | TED Talk. Accessed August 2, 2022. https://www.ted.com/talks/amy_cuddy_your_body_language_may_shape_who_you_are?language=en.

YouTube is a trademark of Google LLC.

Zoom is a trademark of Zoom Video Commuications, Inc.

www.ingramcontent.com/pod-product-compliance
Lightning Source LLC
Chambersburg PA
CBHW070750160726
48004CB00001B/128